FINDING
STRENGTH
in Your Weaknesses

FINDING STRENGTH
in Your Weaknesses

*Turn Your Vulnerabilities
into Your Greatest Testimony*

Christopher D. Ramey

Copyright ©2022, Christopher D. Ramey

All Rights Reserved. This book may not be reproduced in whole or in part without the written consent of the publisher, except by a reviewer who may quote brief passages in a review. Nor may any part of this book be reproduced, stored in a retrieval system, or transmitted in any form or by any means, electronic, mechanical, photocopying, recording, or other, without the written permission of the publisher.

ISBN: 979-8-218-01083-6 (Paperback)
ISBN: 979-8-218-01082-9 (Hardcover)
ISBN: 979-8-218-01084-3 (Ebook)

Cover Design: Style-Matters.com
Cover Imagery: Shutterstock / SergeyIT

To my wife, Sheryl.

My Sweet Pea. My love. You have been one of the greatest blessings God has given me. The love you have shown me throughout the years inspires me beyond words. I will love you and cherish you for the rest of my life. I awake every day, excited for another day to not only serve and glorify God, but to have another day to be your husband. I am so proud of the woman you have become, and I am excited for all of the blessings God has in store for you.

Contents

Introduction	*ix*
1. Finding Strength in Your Transition	1
2. Inviting God into Your Vulnerabilities	15
3. Finding Purpose in Your Storm	27
4. Endure or Submit?	41
5. Conform or Transform?	53
6. Just Keep Going	65
7. Faith in the Valley	77
8. Commit to the Climb	91
9. Your Past Does Not Define Your Future	103
10. Freedom	117
Conclusion	133
Acknowledgments	*141*
About the Author	*147*

Each time he said, my grace is all you need. My power works best in weaknesses. So now I am glad to boast about my weaknesses, so that the power of Christ can work through me. That is why I take pleasure in my weaknesses, and in the insults, hardships, persecutions, and troubles that I suffer for Christ. For when I am weak, then I am strong.

—2 Corinthians 12:9–10

(New Living Translation, NLT)

INTRODUCTION

We live in a world where our vulnerabilities are seen as weaknesses. These weaknesses can often dictate how we see ourselves, and not only that, but they can dictate how we perceive our value with God. For example, we often find ourselves questioning why God loves us if we continue to sin after we have been forgiven? We begin to question how a sinner like ourselves can be used by God. This has been an ongoing battle in my walk of faith, a battle that I often find myself in more times than I would like to be. I fully committed my life to God on April 4, 2021. This is a day that I will remember for the rest of my life as it was the first time I can honestly say I felt the presence of the Holy Spirit. It was Easter Sunday, and I was in quarantine because I had just arrived in Naples, Italy, where I would be stationed for the next three years. It was my last day of quarantine, so I could not physically go out and do what I used to call "the religious check in the box" by attending Easter service. Therefore, I decided to find a sermon online to fulfill my religious "requirement." I remember noticing this pastor on Instagram, and I was intrigued with his style and the way he presented his sermons. The pastor I am referring to is named Michael Todd. He is the lead pastor at Transformation Church in Tulsa, Oklahoma. I thought to myself, "Well, at least I won't be bored. At least this will be an entertaining service." Little did I know that the sermon would be the spark that would change everything.

During the sermon, the pastor spoke about the life he had been delivered from, and I felt as if he was describing my life to me, as if he had a front-row seat to the movie that was the dark life I was living at that time. Let me pause right here and say, you never know how deep and dark a life of sin you are living until you are delivered from it. I was oblivious to the sinful life I was living. I figured that, because I was a good person and was nice to most people, my life couldn't be that bad, right? The conviction that fell upon me brought to light the current life I was living, and it showed me that I was indeed a sinner. I felt the presence of God within my hotel room, in quarantine. There was no one present—no pastor, no church, just the online service, the Holy Spirit, and me. I begin to sob uncontrollably, and I do not mean just a regular cry. I mean the "ugly cry," the type of crying where you cannot even speak words, as if you have become mute. In that moment, I knew it was time to relinquish control. I knew it was time to surrender and submit to God. I knew it was time to repent my sins and accept Jesus Christ as my Lord and Savior. That is exactly what I did on that day, as I celebrated the resurrection of Christ; I myself had been resurrected into a new creation through Jesus Christ.

I have never lived the perfect life. Like many others, I have lived a life full of mistakes, regret, shame, and in times, pure and utter disgust. Yes, you read that correctly: I said disgust. There are things I have done in my life that I should have felt disgusted to do in the moment, but I did not. I felt no remorse for what I was doing. I was enslaved so deeply in sin that I did not recognize I was doing things that were uncharacteristic of my personality or how my upbringing in church should have molded me to be. With that being said, I have come to realize that it is not a structure or a building that shapes us into what God has created us to be. It is the presence of God in our lives that molds, shapes, and transforms us into what He so intimately created us to be. I often think back on the things I have done, and in those moments when I would have previously felt shame, I instead started to develop a sense of joy and a sense of relief. I started to recognize the work that God was doing and the internal changes He was making in my life. It gave me a sense of hope that no matter what was to come, I knew He would be with me. Where there was once fear, there was now courage. Where there was once anxiety there was now peace, a peace that would transcend all peace. This was something I had truly never experienced in my life because I had been placing a high value on emotions that were temporary. What God gives you is eternal. The joy the Holy Spirit gives you is eternal. When it is eternal, it sustains you without expiration. When it is temporary, it only satisfies the current desire of what you think you need in that moment.

You will have noticed that the title of this book is *Finding Strength in Your Weaknesses*. Once I was baptized and had accepted Jesus Christ as my Lord and Savior, everything did change, but it did not become as easy as I thought it would be. I thought all my past sins and desires of the flesh would leave automatically, and yes, most did. However, there was one area of my former life that still tries to imprison me even to this day. That is the sin of sexual desires and lust. More specifically, pornography. In the earlier moments of my new life with Christ I did not understand why I was still being tempted by this. Why did this specific sin arise daily in an attempt to imprison me? I found myself seeking answers, and the Holy Spirit revealed a Scripture to me. This particular Scripture is also the anchor Scripture for this book. In this Scripture, the apostle Paul wrote in 2 Corinthians 12:9–10 (NLT), "Each time he said, my grace is all you need. My power works best in weaknesses. So now I am glad to boast about my weaknesses, so that the power of Christ can work through me. That is why I take pleasure in my weaknesses, and in the insults, hardships, persecutions, and troubles that I suffer for Christ. For when I am weak, then I am strong."

So now I do not see my weaknesses and my vulnerabilities as burdens. I see them as opportunities for God to display His power, and for others to see the work He is doing in me, for His grace is sufficient to fulfill all of my needs and to meet me exactly where I am. God reminded me of this during one of my daily devotionals. The Holy Spirit spoke to me and revealed to me what would be the banner of my life: "You can't celebrate the destination if you don't testify about the journey." He expounded upon this by telling me, "Your vulnerabilities and your burdens will be your greatest testimony," which is the subtitle of this book. I know most books are written to inspire, motivate, and ignite one's desire to ascend above where they currently are emotionally, mentally, and physically. What I am going to give you is complete transparency. I am going to give you real-life accounts of my struggles and how God continues to meet me in those struggles and provide me with the fuel my faith needs to propel me forward in my relationship with Him. I am also going to give you messages that He has given me along the way to shield me amid the storms and spiritual warfare we all face. I am living proof that no matter where you are or what you have done, God can turn your mess into a message and your test into a testimony if you open your heart and allow Him to come in, take control, and do so.

The misconception is that we have to be a refurbished product, with all of the cracks and blemishes in the foundation of who we are, repaired and made new. This misconception hinders people from taking a step in the direction of freedom by salvation through Jesus Christ. I was one of those people and can intimately relate to this. I had this clouded belief about what I thought would have to happen before I could come to Jesus. In reality, it wasn't that I wanted to be a finished product before I came to

Jesus. In all honesty, I just didn't want to sever the ties to the sinful life I had been living. There was always "one more" sinful thing I wanted to accomplish before coming to God. I felt that if I accomplished that one sinful thing, I would be able to freely walk away from it all. This was definitely not the case, as there was a recurring cycle of a common phrase of "one more" sinful thing. It was as if I believed that this one more thing would fulfill my sinful desires. But it was a bottomless abyss that could never be filled. I am thankful that Jesus did not leave me as the one who went astray. I am thankful that He did not allow me to continue to wander astray from the path He created me to walk upon.

Life is a precious gift that I am so thankful God continues to give me. With every day He approves my "wake-up call," it gives me the opportunity to go out and tell others what He has done for me. I am constantly amazed by how good and faithful God is. Just when I think He has done something so amazing in my life, He comes back and tops the last thing. Every breath that comes in and leaves your body is a gift. So the next time you are having a bad day, or you are struggling with that particular thing that has plagued you, I want you to do something for me. I want you to place your hand on your chest and feel your heartbeat. While you are doing this, I also want you to close your eyes and just breathe. In that moment, you will feel life. Every breath you inhale and exhale, and every beat of your heart, is proof that God loves you. He has plans for you, and He preordained for you to be alive at this specific time. From this day forward, when you are dealing with things that seem to overwhelm you, remember that God placed you in this time for a reason.

I hope this book will give hope and peace to someone who may be going through what I have been through in my life. It is my sincerest hope that you will not hide your vulnerabilities, and will instead invite God into your vulnerabilities and allow Him to strengthen you. I pray that God will fill you with His Holy Spirit, and that you will allow Him to manifest within you so that you may grow in the fruits of the spirit that will equip you to endure whatever storm you may be facing. Because it is in our weakness that He does His greatest work, and it is because of this that we can find strength in our weaknesses. It is in the promises of God that every place that was once broken will be restored. For God brings life to things that are lifeless, and He will deliver you from whatever it is that you are going through. Trust in Him, and He will see you through it. There is nothing that can stand against you if God is for you and with you.

So be strong and courageous!
Do not be afraid and do not panic
before them. For the Lord your God will
personally go ahead of you.
He will neither fail you nor abandon you.

—Deuteronomy 31:6 (NLT)

CHAPTER 1

Finding Strength in Your Transition

Once I received salvation I felt like a new person. I started to recognize changes instantaneously. As the apostle Paul wrote in 2 Corinthians 5:17 (NLT), "This means anyone who belongs to Christ has become a new person. The old life is gone; a new life has begun!" However, in the days to come, I would discover that yes, I had a new life. Yes, I was a new creation because I had accepted Jesus Christ as my Lord and Savior. But I was not where I thought I would be. I was no longer the person I had been, but I was also not who I was created to be. It was in these moments when I first learned about transition. A simple way to define "transition" is as a process or a period of changing from one state or condition to another. We are all in constant transition, whether we are going from one job to another, moving from one city to another, or shifting from an old way of life into a new way of living. There is no transition without a process. The process is when God will begin to shape, mold, and reform you into what He created you to be, so you can serve in the calling He has placed on your life. Imagine a potter shaping and molding clay. The potter works the clay with clear direction and precision toward what he is intending to create. The process is pure, fluent, and seemingly effortless. If you allow yourself to be clay on the wheel of the Master Potter, He will create a masterpiece of righteousness and purity. The beauty of His work will be seen by others as they will recognize the transformation you have undergone. Therefore, be clay—a substance that is easy to form and mold—and do not allow yourself to become hardened as stone. The process to reshape and transform a block of stone is a much more arduous task and is a much slower process. Submission to the process of work determines the process of your transformation. If you submit to the Master Potter, He will transform you into what He created you to be.

This process does not go unchallenged. It is in this process when we are at our most vulnerable. You are subject to attack when you are at your most vulnerable state. Vulnerabilities expose our weakest parts. Look at it this way: you would not attack an enemy when they are at their full strength and are prepared for an attack. You have a higher chance of success if you wait until they are vulnerable and unaware of the pending attack. The enemy will constantly attack us in the process to either redirect us to our old ways of living, or to simply force us to pause in the process. It is important to know that when you pause in the process, there is no progress. And where there is no progress, there is no development. What the enemy fears most is the day when you will figure out who you are in Christ and who you were created to be. I am in my process of transition, and I find myself in spiritual warfare daily.

The enemy tries to imprison my mind with past sins I have committed. He uses this tactic as an attempt to redirect me, as if he is trying to show me that I am missing the best parts of my life. I no longer wish to indulge in the sins of sexual desire. I no longer wish to have sexual escapades with women whom I do not intend on committing to but would only seek them out for temporary satisfaction.

In my former life I was like most people. I wanted immediate satisfaction. I wanted to satisfy my desires without any thought of the long-term consequences they would have on my life. I didn't even think about seeking something that would sustain me. When you continue to seek immediate satisfaction, it will only ease your desires temporarily, which will result in you repeating the same actions and becoming imprisoned in a never-ending cycle of fulfilling yourself with temporary satisfaction. This is how the enemy arms himself for battle against me. He equips himself with arrows of lust in the hope of penetrating the hedge of protection that God has placed around me. He attempts to lure me in with thoughts of past relationships and pornographic images that would cause me to drift back into a life of sin. He constantly searches for gaps or missing pieces in the "armor" of God that we, as believers, are to equip ourselves with. The Scriptures say, in Ephesians 6:13–18 (NLT):

> Therefore, put on every piece of God's armor so you will be able to resist the enemy in the time of evil. Then after the battle you will still be standing firm. Stand your ground, putting on the belt of truth and the body armor of God's righteousness. In addition to all of these, hold up the shield of faith to stop the fiery arrows of the devil. Put on salvation as your helmet, and take the sword of the Spirit, which is the word of God. Pray in the Spirit at all times and on every occasion. Stay alert and be persistent in your prayers for all believers everywhere. For shoes, put on the peace that comes from the Good News so that you will be fully prepared.

Equipping ourselves with the full armor of God is how we ready ourselves for attacks from the enemy. The most important thing to remember is that the battle is not yours. This was an early mistake of mine. I would not only try to defend my mind and spirit from the oncoming onslaught of attacks, but I would also try to fight back by resisting temptation on my own strength, instead of seeking strength from God to endure. I found myself failing and drifting deeper and deeper into the abyss of sin, uncertain of how I would escape from the chains that I kept finding myself bound by. Let me pause right here and say that God will supply a way out, and He will never place any burden on you that you cannot manage. It is because of this that we ignore all the exits the Holy Spirit illuminates for us. We step past the boundaries and continue to dive deeper into a battle that we have put ourselves in. Make no mistake, spiritual warfare is a very real thing, but there are times when we are engaging in battles that we have placed ourselves in. For example, we resist temptation that we have brought upon ourselves by going to that Instagram profile and looking at that post that we should not have looked at. One look would trigger a sinful desire that could cause us to act out, and this creates a domino effect that leads us right back to the very thing God delivered us from.

The Holy Spirit comes to convict the world of sin, righteousness, and the coming judgment (John 16:8 [NLT]). In those moments when you find yourself drifting, the Holy Spirit will convict you of the sin you are drifting back into. I personally view this as a defense mechanism that redirects me before I drift too far away. An analogy I can use to break this down further would be sailing on a boat that is out to sea and is dragging anchor. You become aware of what is happening because you notice the drifting and movement of the boat. Therefore, you drop your anchor again to reaffirm your position and decrease your drift. Similarly, the Holy Spirit gives you warnings that you are moving too far away, so you can drop your anchor again to hold you in place. It is also important to address what you are anchored to and how strong your anchor is. Anchors are created from an exceptionally durable and sturdy metal. The most overlooked part of the anchor is the anchor chain. Anchor chains must be extremely durable because they are the connecting link between the ship and the anchor. So what are you connecting to your anchor? If your anchor is Jesus Christ, how are you connecting to

Him? Are you spending time reading your Bible? Are you talking to God and seeking His guidance and direction? Are you allowing the Holy Spirit to take control and lead you to where God wants you to be? It is important that we not only ensure we have a strong anchor, but that we ensure that the chain which connects us to our anchor is strong as well.

When our eyes are focused on God, we can tune out the distractions around us. We can move forward in the promises God has for us and continue to move forward in our transition. It is when we take our focus off of God that we begin to waver in our walk of faith. Faith is the fuel that keeps you moving forward. When your car is low on fuel it only has a limited distance that it can travel. We are not so different in this aspect, as it relates to what we are filling ourselves up with. We will only be able to travel the journey God has placed before us for a limited distance if we are not filling ourselves up with the presence of God. If we are not growing in His word and fueling our faith, we will not be filled with the right fuel and we will not be able to persevere throughout life's difficulties.

For all things are possible if you have faith and believe (Matthew 19:26 [NLT]).

Let me give you an example. When Jesus Christ called out to the disciples to meet Him on the water, this seemed like an impossible task. No one had ever walked on water in biblical history until this point. One disciple displayed faith so strong that he was able to momentarily do the impossible because his eyes were focused on Jesus. When Peter stepped out of the boat with his eyes fixed on Jesus, he was able to take a couple of steps (Matthew 14:25–29 [NLT]). Pretty amazing, right? However, most people will automatically focus on the negative by saying, "Didn't Peter sink underwater?" They overlook the fact that he showed a tremendous amount of faith by taking steps toward what others saw as an impossible task. Fix your eyes on the one who sustains you and all things become possible. It was not until Peter took his focus off of Jesus Christ that he began to sink. His lack of focus resulted in a lack of faith. If your eyes are focused on Jesus throughout your transition, you will begin to take steps—even strides which those around you may see as impossible. Remain in faith and allow your life to be a testimony not of the impossible, but of the fact that all things are possible with faith in He who is the God of unlimited possibilities.

Your weakness does not define how Christ sees you. He sees your weakness as an opportunity for you to connect with others. When you empathize with other people who may share the same struggles as you, or who may just be having a tough time, you are able to use your weaknesses to connect with them. You never know how profound this can be for someone who may feel isolated and alone in their vulnerabilities. That is what vulnerabilities do; if left unaddressed, they will consume you and develop a mirage within your mind that tells you that you are the only one who is having a tough time. There is freedom in connecting with others through your vulnerabilities. Strength is found in freedom because it takes strength to reveal those things that you have never shared with anyone, the things you are afraid that if anyone ever found out, you would

> **Your weakness does not define how Christ sees you.**

be cast away into an even deeper isolation than your vulnerabilities already have you currently dwelling in. So I encourage you to allow yourself to share and connect with someone with whom you have developed a level of trust. It is important to remain in fellowship with not only God, but with others as well.

We need to see our transition for what it is! It is not a prison sentence or a never-ending cycle of attacks and uncertainties. Within the word "transition" we also find "transit." When you are in transition you are in transit to where God wants to take you. Find joy in your transition! You are moving closer and closer to your calling and to who God created you to be. While you are going through the storms that you often meet in your transition, it is important to not pass through without seeing the revelation within each storm. The basic explanation of a revelation is the making known of something that was previously secret or unknown. Sometimes God will take you through a storm to reveal something to you, what He put in you, and to give you spiritual strength. So go forth in boldness by remembering that your vulnerabilities do not define your strength. For your strength comes from the God who created you.

I do not know the genesis of your story, but the sins of your former life do not dictate your exodus. We all know Genesis and Exodus to be the first two books in the Bible. The names of those chapters have specific meanings. Genesis simply means "in the beginning." Its name was derived from the opening words of the text. Exodus simply means "a going out; a departure or emigration," usually in reference to a mass departure or exit of many people. Therefore, if I were to use these terms to describe the process of our transition, our genesis would be salvation. Our exodus would be stepping out of our former lives into what God has called us to be. The sins that were washed away during your rebirth in Christ do not dictate the amount of grace that is given to you. Grace is a gift from God, and it is freely given to those who accept Jesus Christ as their Lord and Savior. However, our transition is a period in our spiritual lives when we will slip, and sometimes we will fall. Find joy and rejoice in knowing that God's grace and mercy is new every day. It does not run out of stock, nor does it need to be replenished. It is everlasting and eternal, just as our God is. Your genesis, as well as your exodus, will be beautiful masterpieces if you allow God to be the sole artist.

Come to me, all of you who are weary and carry heavy burdens, and I will give you rest.

—Matthew 11:28 (NLT)

CHAPTER 2

Inviting God into Your Vulnerabilities

I did not have the model childhood that most children have. I grew up with a single parent and lived with my grandparents until I was sixteen years old. My mother did the best she could and worked hard all her life. And with the help of my grandparents, she was able to give me the best possible upbringing she could. I did not have the typical household with a mother and a father, but there were people who stepped in and filled those roles in my life. My father, whom I have never met, abandoned my mother when she was in labor with me. Sounds bad, right? Surprisingly, I grew up without ever feeling animosity toward my father or his family. In all honesty, I had moments during my early childhood years when I was at least curious as to whether I would ever meet him. Would he ever reach out to me and at least see if I was doing OK? Or would he ever check to see if I was alive, for that matter? How could he have a son and not want to communicate with him?

As I grew older, I still did not know why he had left, and I felt like I could not blame him because of it. There were reasons that were unknown to me and my family as to why he could not remain in our lives. I could have surrendered to normal behaviors that are often present during situations like this. I could have let anger consume me and control my life. Because when something or someone can control your emotions, they can also control you. I had to make decisions early in my life that would dictate the very direction it would take. Would I surrender to the normal patterns of society and remain a victim? Or would I let this circumstance empower me? Would I allow the disappointments of my father's absence to become the compass of my life that would dictate the very direction my life would take? No, I would not become a slave to my circumstance, and I would not allow someone else's decision to dictate my emotional vulnerabilities.

Sounds like I had life all figured out, right? Yeah, I thought so too, but I was wrong. Regardless of how I chose to manage the situation with my father, I did not realize the internal impact it would have on me. I was not serving God during this part of my life. Yes, I would attend church, but only because it was a requirement in my household. What I perceived to be a nontraumatic experience was the spark that would ignite events in my life that I would not be able to overcome with my own strength. There was anger and commitment issues that had remained dormant within me until my teenage years when the effects began to become visible. This led to me being exposed to pornographic material as I believed that no relationship could work because it would only be a matter of time before any partner would leave me, just like my father had. This developed into an addiction that

I was oblivious too for many years. It also guided my perspective on how much I thought people loved me. This is a very toxic way of thinking, and it can have spiritual effects for many of us. If we do not think people whom we can see will not love us, then how can we have faith and believe that God loves us?

During the earlier parts of my walk of faith I would momentarily revert to sin but would quickly repent and continue moving forward. I wondered why I was still struggling with sin. I had an unreal expectation of what I thought a life submitted to God would look like. This unreal expectation took me down a dark path. There were times when I struggled to remain faithful and free of sin. I would find myself sitting on the floor in my bedroom and wondering, "Why, God, are you allowing this to happen to me?" I felt so distant from God, and in those moments I was begging for Him to speak to me, but I would hear nothing. It was not because He was absent, because He was always present. It was because of the negative seeds I was planting within myself. I was drowning out His voice with clouds of doubt and unfaithfulness. It was like a deep fog had blinded me to all the ways He was trying to speak to me. I was sinking in a quicksand of discouragement. The more I moved and tried to persevere on my own strength, the deeper I would sink. I went to work one day and my friend Jasmine Smith stopped me when I walked into the office. She said to me, "God told me to tell you not to be discouraged." This breathed new life into me; it reminded me that He had never left my side. It also cause me to wonder how long He had been trying to tell me this. I had been nourishing every negative seed that was planted within me to be harvested and take root. I had let branches of doubt grow around my spirit, creating a barrier that would not allow me to reach Him.

You must be careful of what you allow to dwell within you. You must be conscious of what seeds you plant within yourself, whether it's seeds of negativity (such as anger, lust, anxiety, or depression) or seeds of positivity (like hope, peace, joy, and love). We cannot expect our lives to bear positive fruit when we only plant negative seeds. Therefore, how can one expect to manifest and grow in the fruits of the spirit when they are planting seeds of the flesh? What you plant within yourself will take root and grow into your identity, and what you identify with will give you a transparent account of what is controlling your life. God cannot correct what you will not allow Him to dwell in. God does not just want the good parts of you and the things that bring you immense pride. He also wants the vulnerable and weakest parts of you. Therefore, invite God into your weaknesses and vulnerabilities. Allow Him to enter and dwell in those places because those are the very places where He will tell the greatest story about your life. The Holy Spirit spoke to me this morning and said, "If you let God be the author of your story, the words that are written of your life will be living testimonies to lost souls who are spiritually dead. They will be resurrected by the power of the Holy Spirit who will work in and through you to revive a spirit that was created to be in communion with God." So let your story be written. Let God be the author of the testimony of your life that will bring spiritual freedom to imprisoned souls.

He loves you so much and He wants to be in communion with you. No matter what you have done or where you have been, I encourage you to not walk alone in your struggles. You do not have to be extraordinary or do extraordinary things to be loved. I will share this Scripture from Matthew 3:15–17 (NLT) as an example: "But Jesus said, 'It should be done, for we must carry out all that God requires. Or for we must fulfill all righteousness.' So John agreed to baptize him. After his baptism, as Jesus came up out of the water, the heavens were opened, and he saw the Spirit of God descending like a dove and settling on him. And a voice from heaven said, 'This is my dearly loved Son, who brings me great joy.'" I want to bring your attention to the last section of the Scripture, "This is my dearly loved Son, who brings me great joy." God professed His love for Jesus before He performed a single miracle, before He did any of the extraordinary works He would go on to complete during His purpose.

You do not have to have it all together to be loved by God. Genuine love requires no amazing tasks or obligation to be fulfilled. It only seeks love in return. For the Scriptures say in 1 John 4:15–16 (NLT), "We know how much God loves us, and we have put our trust in his love.

God is love, and all who live in love live in God, and God lives in them. All who declare that Jesus is the Son of God have God living in them, and they live in God." His love never wavers, it is constant and never changes. God is the same yesterday, today, and forever. So is His love for His children. Take a deeper look at this from a different perspective. The relationships you have, whether they are in marriage, courtship, or friendship, are sustained by genuine love. All parties choose to remain in these relationships because they have love for one another. When you choose someone, the love is genuine. You are chosen by God. His love for you is genuine, and no matter what you do, it will never change. Accept the love He has for you by lowering the barrier around your vulnerabilities. You do not have to hide who you are from Him. You do not have to be a finished product or completely cleansed of all unrighteousness. He wants you to come to Him just as you are. Come to Him with all your weaknesses and vulnerabilities, and allow Him to shower you with grace and love. Take His hand and allow Him to walk with you through all aspects of your life, including the days that are full of light and the days when it seems the darkness will never end.

I know there are times when you just want to give up. I know that the life you walked away from when you gave your life to God was much easier to live because you were free to do what you wanted. There was no shame when you sinned, and there was no sadness when you felt like you had let God down. We live in a world where easy is perceived as a good thing. I mean, who wants things to be difficult, right? Wouldn't it just be easy to revert to my sinful life when I did not see the weakest parts of me as vulnerabilities? However, all freedom is not truly freedom. When we freely commit sin, it imprisons us back in the very chains that God freed us from. Sin cripples our faith and hope, and shame blinds us to grace. In those times when you feel like you cannot go any farther, you have to remember to seek peace from the One who sacrificed His life for you, the One who loved you so much that He gave His life so that you could be redeemed and in good standing with His father. Jesus said in Matthew 11:28 (NLT), "Come to me, all of you who are weary and carry heavy burdens, and I will give you rest." So do not let shame become the storm in your life where you are cast out into deep waters without vision of escape due to the rains of despair that shower over you. You have peace in Jesus; He is the peace in the middle of your storm. He calms the winds and waves with the sound of His voice. There is no storm which He cannot rescue you from if you take refuge in Him.

> **In those times when you feel like you cannot go any farther, you have to remember to seek peace from the One who sacrificed His life for you.**

It was not until I surrendered and allowed Jesus to become my true north that I fully realized the feeling of peace. When I gave God control over my life through the power of the Holy Spirit to navigate the direction of my path, I started to notice changes He was making in my life. Freedom was no longer a temporary glimpse or snapshot of what I hoped for. It started to become an unclouded vision of grace. Now, whenever I see the storm on the horizon, I know I can turn to Jesus and

He will shower me with His peace. This is the starting point when you release control. God cannot effectively restore the broken parts of you if you are battling Him for control over your life. We ask God to be the source of our strength and faith, but we will not allow Him to be the source of our direction and decisions. The enemy wants us to become complacent and satisfied with our current circumstances. Complacency breeds destruction that makes way for distractions from what God has assigned you to do. That feeling of satisfaction that you feel is guided by the enemy and is meant to redirect your attention away from seeking God and allowing Him to lead your life. My prayer for you is that you will allow God to meet you in your vulnerabilities and replace what was once seen as a weakness with His unwavering peace and strength. I pray that you will have faith that He will give you the mind, heart, and vision to seek and see Him in all aspects of life. In the name of my Lord and Savior Jesus Christ, Amen.

Dear brothers and sisters, when troubles of any kind come your way, consider it an opportunity for great joy. For you know that when your faith is tested, your endurance has a chance to grow. So let it grow, for when your endurance is fully developed, you will be perfect and complete, needing nothing.

—James 1:2–4 (NLT)

CHAPTER 3

Finding Purpose in Your Storm

I grew up in Mississippi, and I currently own a home in Florida. Living in these areas, I have seen my fair share of storms throughout my life. When there is a hurricane on the horizon, it is quite common for the people living in the surrounding areas to go to their local stores to prepare in case there is a loss of power or other unforeseen circumstances. As the saying goes, "prepare for the worst," and that is what most people do. It is the fear of the unknown that causes people to wipe out a grocery store and buy things they would not normally buy. After all the planning and preparation, the predicted hurricane often turns out to be just a tropical storm. We place our trust in a meteorologist who is telling us what is to come, but often we will not step out on faith and believe God for what He says is coming. This is because we allow the storm that is around us to drown out His voice and direction.

There is something to be said about this and there is a message within this. Fear of the unknown causes you to do things that are uncharacteristic of your true self. Make no mistake, preparing yourself for things that are beyond your control is a wise decision, but how are you preparing yourself? Are you allowing faith to be the foundation of your preparations? Or is it fear that is the foundation of your preparations? Have you been out with your family or running errands when you noticed that it looked as if severe weather was imminent? The first thought that comes to your mind may be, "I need to get home as soon as possible before it starts to rain." Your focus has shifted from your current task to seeking shelter as soon as possible. This redirection often comes from fear. For example, you may be fearful of how others will drive during severe weather and how that could cause a vehicular accident. Fear is a false emotion that arises in response to the unknown. Fear causes us to retreat from things that may not exist, but we have allowed it to entrap our minds. Where our minds lead our bodies will follow. What you allow to enter your mind will manifest and grow within your mind. Once it has been planted, it will eventually reach your heart and cause you to seek shelter in the very place God brought you out of.

If you allow the uncomfortable feeling of fear to fix your vision on things that do not exist, it will change your course back to what you deem as comfortable. Comfortability can be a good thing—if you find comfort in the right thing. In this case, the comfortability I am speaking of is our past sinful lives. Before finding the conviction of the Holy Spirit that provides us with the revelation of our sinful lives, we find comfort in the impure freedom of sin. This impure freedom and comfort are the culprits of why we cannot escape the depths of sin on our own power. Therefore, when life gets uncomfortable and we enter seasons of our lives that are uncertain, the enemy will use this against us to drive us back to our sinful lives. Do not submit to the lie from the father of lies that tells you that sin is a better place to dwell in than the new season God is taking you to. In this case, it is good to be uncomfortable because with comfort comes complacency. If you are comfortable then you are not progressing. Find pride in the discomfort because you are progressing and maturing on your spiritual journey of progressive sanctification. No matter what storm you may find yourself in, remember the Lord who created and has dominion over all things is with you during it.

The storms we face in life have a purpose. According to James 1:2–4 (NLT), "Dear brothers and sisters, when troubles of any kind come your way, consider it an opportunity for great joy. For you know that when your faith is tested, your endurance has a chance to grow. So let it grow, for when your endurance is fully developed, you will be perfect and complete, needing nothing." Running cannot become the default choice we revert to when there seems to be trouble on the horizon. Do not only find joy in your purpose but also find joy in your storm. Finding joy within your storm will bring you clarity and will lift the fog of doubt that surrounds your heart and mind. When your heart and mind are open to the direction of God, you will be able to move through troubled waters with peace if the Prince of Peace is what you are anchored to. He who speaks and calms the winds of the storm will not allow the storm to overtake you. Instead of looking around at the crashing waves of fear and despair, focus on the calming voice and presence of God.

Do not allow the unknowns within your storm to cause you to flee and run in the opposite direction from where God is trying to take you. When we are troubled, we only need to seek peace in the presence of God. How you live dictates how you move. If you live in fear, you will walk in fear. If you live in faith, you will walk in faith. Running means chaos is imminent, but walking means peace is present. Running represents urgency and walking represents patience. Running means that you are trying to escape something. Walking means that you have already been freed from something. The storms that you are currently in will strengthen you and develop you for a season God is calling you into. However, you cannot go through the spiritual metamorphosis to become what God is transforming you into if you keep running away and seeking shelter instead of enduring and remaining faithful. He cannot prepare you to withstand the hurricane if you retreat from the tropical storm. How can we expect to withstand a challenging season of our lives if we run from the slightest drizzle of rain? When you learn to withstand the rain, you can endure the pain. Pain brings life to your purpose, and adversity will revive the gifts that are dormant within you.

In God we take refuge, and His Holy Spirit will comfort us in our times of need. Therefore, stand bold during your storm, for God did not give His children a spirit of fear. If He be for us, it does not matter who or what is against us. What if I were to tell you that there are cases in which He is trying to give you a revelation out of the disasters that consume every aspect of your life? What if the very thing that is broken is being broken by Him because it is the only way He can free you from the thing that causes you to drift further into the storm than He intended? What if the job you lost was taking time away from God and your family? What if He is removing you from that job because He has something better for you? You must pray and learn to seek God everywhere and in everything. If you are not seeking His presence and drawing near to Him, you will miss what He is trying to show you. His plan for your life may not align with your outlook for your life. Therefore, having trust and faith is essential on your path of development.

This is something I have learned to do throughout my walk of faith. I can tell you that God has shown me things in ways that I did not think was possible, and He linked them to biblical Scripture for confirmation. For example, during a work trip in Scotland, the Holy Spirit reminded me of a movie called *Cast Away*, starring Tom Hanks. In this movie, the protagonist's plane goes down during a storm, and he manages to survive the crash. He eventually arrives at an uninhabited island and immediately tries to adapt to his surroundings to ensure his survival. This is what the Holy Spirit was trying to show me. It is not only important to endure or survive the storm, but you must also know what you will do next. Will you be content with managing to get by or merely survive the wave of disappointments that formed the hurricane that was a period of your life? Or will you continue to press forward? The main character in the movie could have given up; instead, he tries multiple times to escape the island, even though he fails repeatedly. The important thing is that he is learning from each failure, and he approaches the next attempt differently than before, until eventually he escapes the island. He never quits, regardless of how impossible the task seems. He finds purpose, and that gives him the strength he needs to escape.

If there was a billboard for a biblical character who could be the poster child of "I am going through hardships in my life but I am still going to serve God," the apostle Paul would be that person. He was beaten, imprisoned, shipwrecked, and persecuted—but the one thing that remained constant in his life was that he served God through it all. He wrote parts of the New Testament while in prison. During imprisonment he was still serving

God and edifying the body of Christ. Immediately after the Holy Spirit spoke to me using the movie *Cast Away*, He immediately drew my attention to the Acts of the Apostles, specifically chapters 27 and 28. To give you context, Paul was a prisoner on a boat that was en route to Rome where he was to stand trial. During this voyage, a storm raged against the ship and crew. In a circumstance when most would only think of themselves and their own survival, Paul was still committed to serving and being used by God.

You will move with courage and not succumb to fear when purpose is the path you follow. The Acts of the Apostles 27:21–25 (NLT) says, "No one had eaten for a long time. Finally, Paul called the crew together and said, 'Men, you should have listened to me in the first place and not left Crete. You would have avoided all this damage and loss. But take courage! None of you will lose your lives, even though the ship will go down. For last night, an angel of the God to whom I belong and whom I serve stood beside me, and he said, 'Do not be afraid, Paul, for you will surely stand trial before Caesar! What is more,

God in His goodness has granted safety to everyone sailing with you.' So take courage! For I believe God. It will be just as he said.'" Paul was not just committed to surviving the storm; he was committed to walking in his purpose and serving God.

You would think that after being shipwrecked and making it safely to shore, the trouble would be over, right? While Paul was trying to build a fire, a snake bit him. However, no harm came to him and he simply shook the snake from his arm. At this point he could have just given up and remained in the chains that imprisoned him. Not only did he remain faithful and keep serving, but he went on to heal the townspeople. Never did he waver in his faith or his commitment to serving God. When you are committed to your purpose and serving God, there is no storm that will cause you to drift from what God has called you to do. What if we commit to our purpose instead of retreating to the life we were freed from? We all stumble and fall short of God's glory. The stumble or the fall does not dictate what happens next; you do. You can either keep moving forward in purpose or dwell in the storm.

Sometimes all it takes to find your purpose is to walk in faith. What if the thing that is keeping you from your purpose is a lack of faith? Faith can be the very thing that propels you into a season of overflow. Or the lack of faith can be the very thing that causes you to miss the blessings God has for you. You cannot walk in your purpose if you do not have faith. Your purpose will take you to places you may not understand or had never thought you would be in. It will not only take faith to pursue your purpose fearlessly because you trust in God's plans and purposes He has placed on your life, but it will also take faith to remain in your purpose—especially when it does not turn out to be what you thought it would. Because without faith you will go back to what brought you comfort and will not pursue what makes you uncomfortable. This is what purpose is; it is stepping into a new season to serve in the way that

> **Sometimes all it takes to find your purpose is to walk in faith.**

God created you to serve, with the gifts He has given you through His Holy Spirit who determines the gifts that each believer will have (1 Corinthians 12:11 [NLT]). I made up my mind that I will serve God and trust Him, no matter where He takes me. During my daily prayers I make it a point to say to God, "Yes, to whatever it is You want to do in my life. You don't even have to reveal it to me. The answer is already yes." This has empowered me to trust God in all aspects of my life. It gives me peace to totally surrender to His will and purpose for my life.

It allows me to focus and prepare to serve when I reach the destination because I do not have to concern myself with the journey as I know He will lead me through it. When you are not distracted by the storm you can focus on the purpose of the storm. You are so close to your purpose. Do not give up, just keep going forward in faith and allow God to be your shelter from the storm. God, I pray that You will cover whoever is reading this with Your peace and shelter them in Your presence. Give them the strength to endure the storm, and the mind, heart, and vision to see the revelation You are giving them within the storm. I pray that you fill their lives with Your favor and continue to do a supernatural working within them so they can serve in the purpose that You created them to serve in. I love You, I trust You, and I claim in faith that Your children will be covered with Your presence and You will fill them with Your Holy Spirit increasingly each day. It is in the name of my Lord and Savior Jesus Christ I pray, Amen.

He sang: "The Lord is my rock, my fortress, and my Savior; my God is my rock, in whom I find protection. He is my shield, the power that saves me, and my place of safety. He is my refuge, my Savior, the one who saves me from violence. I called on the Lord, who is worthy of praise, and he saved me from my enemies."

—2 Samuel 22:2–4 (NLT)

CHAPTER 4

Endure or Submit?

Oftentimes fear will cause us to retreat to what we consider as "shelter." What is your shelter? What is the thing or the place you look for when your emotions cause turmoil within you? Pornography was my escape; it was the avenue I would travel to unplug from my emotions. It would temporarily numb my senses to what I was currently facing. It became the morphine that would medicate the emotional wounds that were invisible to all but me. It was an escape to an isolated place in my mind that would erase the troubles of my day. Instead of seeking God and bringing my problems to Him, I gave them to porn instead. I figured it would take away the anxieties that plagued me like a sickness and would relapse on a daily occurrence. I thought porn would be the restoration I had been looking for. The only thing I received was a quick fix, like a drug addict I was bound to repeat the same cycle repeatedly. I thought it would bring me solace, but it became my prison. I was blind to the cage I had built around myself and oblivious to the chains I was shackled within. When you allow your weaknesses to control your mind, the truth is hidden within the lies you see. I thought I was free, but I was trapped. I thought I was whole, but I was broken. I was not enduring the storms I was facing; I was submitting to them. The darkness I was imprisoned in became my residence, and the sin I was engulfed in became my identity.

What you identify as can become an idol in your life. Porn became an idol to me. It was the first thing I did when I got home from a long day of work. It was what I retreated to when I was mentally drained from the troubles of my day. I did not seek God or community with other people. I did not want to be around others for any extended period. I would rather continue in the sinful life I was living instead of developing meaningful healthy relationships with others. The fantasy became a reality to me. It was a lie that became a truth, and the truth was that it was damaging all aspects of my life. I could not see the harm it was doing to me. It was as if my vision of the truth was tarnished by the spectacles of sin I was looking through, and they were projecting the lies the enemy had rooted deep within me. Instead of filling my mind with the truth, I was allowing the father of lies to pollute my mind. When the author of lies implants his manuscript of lies within your mind, you begin to live the lie he is scribing within you. It is said that the truth can set you free, but how can you see the truth if sin is what has consumed your vision? Conviction can restore your vision. The Holy Spirit came to convict the world of sin, righteousness, and the coming judgment (John 16:8 [NLT]).

It was the conviction of the Holy Spirit that restored my sight and convicted me of the sinful life I was living. It is the Holy Spirit that finds us in our darkest places and brings us to the door of salvation. It is not until you allow the One who leads in all truth to lead you to the truth, way, and the life, that you will be able to finally see the truth. A lie cannot come from the source of truth. Jesus Christ is the source of truth; He is the word made flesh (John 1:14 [NLT]). Because if grace is the essence of salvation, then truth is the compass that will lead you to Jesus Christ. When you surrender to God the lies will begin to fade like storm clouds giving way to the sun. His light will begin to illuminate the darkest parts of your life by cleansing you of the blemishes of sin that have stained your spirit. One morning, the Holy Spirit spoke to me and said, "It is not only your sinful nature that causes sin, but it is also the fear of enduring." When you endure something, it is not something that is over quickly. For when you endure you suffer patiently, and it is something that remains in existence for an extended period.

It is the Holy Spirit that finds us in our darkest places and brings us to the door of salvation.

What I have learned throughout my journey is that fear was a common factor in my submission to sin. The difficulties of enduring something that we struggle with can often develop fear of the battle to come and fear of being in it for extended periods or short but frequent periods of time. It is out of this fear that we are most likely to submit to the very temptations we are trying to resist. Subconsciously we believe that it will be much easier to submit and ease the stress than to resist temptation and endure all that is to come during the journey. It is also our lack of patience that increases the difficulties of enduring the journey. We become tired of the struggle and just want it to be over. We want to be free of the temptations that plague us. Spiritual warfare and temptation can seem like a never-ending nightmare, an unwinnable battle that you must repeat daily.

God's presence is the shield that we need to protect us from the attacks of the enemy. The walls of His presence will protect us from the infinite attacks. He is our rock, our fortress, and our deliverer. In Him we take refuge (2 Samuel 22:2–4 [NLT]). Have faith in knowing that God will be with you throughout it all. For without faith, you will sink in the quicksand of discouragement and it will consume every part of you. The more you struggle to free yourself in quicksand, the faster you will sink. However, if you remain calm, the process of sinking is slowed. Peaceful and calm movements increase your chances to free yourself. How we choose to medicate ourselves can be a dangerous thing. We would rather use a temporary euphoric emotion as an escape instead of allowing our faith and self-control to be what fuels us to endure. A temporary sensation or emotion feels good only for a moment, and it can be the very thing that causes you to be separated from God. So you must ask yourself, "Is a temporary feeling worth jeopardizing my eternal status?"

The obvious answer would be no, but that is not how addiction works. Instead, it makes the escape so much more appealing regardless of the long-term consequences. To be addicted is to continuously submit to a thing despite the harmful consequences or long-lasting changes. This is exactly what the enemy wants. The longer you are drowning in the depths of sin, the longer it will take for God to take you where He wants to take you. Sin can paralyze your development if you allow it to trespass and pervert what is righteous. Do not prolong your development by temporarily filling yourself in the process with the desires of the flesh. Your body is not your own; your body is the temple and dwelling place of the Holy Spirit. The Holy Spirit spoke to me and said, "Your body is my temple. Don't desecrate my temple by allowing sin to enter righteous places." After He spoke this to me, He began to highlight certain words to me, which were: "desecrate," "sanctity," "Godliness," "pious," "inviolability," and "trespass."

To desecrate means to violate the sanctity of, or to treat disrespectfully, irreverently, or outrageously. Sanctity is the holiness of life and character which is Godliness. It is also the quality or state of being holy or sacred, which is inviolability. Godliness is divine, pious, and devout. Piety is marked by or showing reverence for deity and devotion to divine worship. Inviolability is marked by being secure from violation, profanation, assault, or trespass. To trespass is to enter without permission; it is a sin or an offense. The reason I encountered so many moments of weakness was because I was allowing sin to trespass into a place it was not welcomed to reside in. We were born into sin, but we were not created to remain in sin. Therefore, sin trespasses when it enters you because your body was never created to be its residence. Sin violates holy places if it is allowed to take root and dwell. Darkness cannot dwell in the same place as light, just as the spirit of the flesh cannot dwell in the same place as the Holy Spirit. We all have seen houses that have "No Trespassing" signs posted by the owners. I am sure we have all known someone who has had such a sign posted in their yard. Similarly, there are also those who will not allow visitors to enter their residence unless they've called ahead of the visit.

If we are this secure with things that are manufactured by man such as our homes, why can't we be this secure when it comes to what we allow to enter the temple of the Holy Spirit? You secure what you deem valuable. So what is more valuable to you? If you are in it for the long game and are surrendered to God, you will have to endure the tests and temptations that will come your way. If you are to endure and not submit, you must place a "No Trespassing" sign on your spirit and not allow sin to enter and pollute what is meant to be pure. You must guard the door and not allow free admission to the triggers that awaken the flesh. If you are indulging yourself with things that you know will revive that part of you that submits to sin, you are inflicting yourself with wounds from a battle you've placed yourself in. I did this more times than I can count. I was opening the gate and letting the armies of temptation storm the fortress that I was asking God to build around my spirit to shield me from the very attacks I was seeking freedom from.

I was letting the Trojan horse into the city, but the only difference was that I knew what was inside the horse. I knew the very thing that was waiting to attack. Not only did I know, but I also opened the trapdoors to the horse and welcomed the temptation in. There was no illusion, no smoke and mirrors. I knew that if I looked at certain posts on Instagram or watched a particular scene in a movie when I should have changed the channel it would fuel my curiosity, and my curiosity of the unseen would develop a trigger in my imagination. Then I would search for images or posts that were like what I had seen, and I would be lead back down the path to sin. The next step you must do is recognize your triggers. And once you have recognized them, you must then invite God into them and ask Him to use those areas for His purpose. Therefore, you will take what the enemy meant to use against you for evil and instead use it to serve His will. You may think you know what your triggers are, but I encourage you to dig deeper. I thought I knew what my triggers were, but it was the Holy Spirit who revealed to me what my true triggers were. The enemy will hide what truly triggers you behind false triggers he has embedded in your mind to keep you trapped in sin. When you find what triggers you, you can be set free from it if you give it to God.

Now I am not fearful of enduring. For if I am enduring, my faith is building endurance (James 1:2–4 [NLT]). When you have endurance, you can bear an unpleasant, arduous process or situation without giving way. A life submitted to Christ is a marathon that requires endurance. This is not a relay race or a sprint that will be over quickly. It is a process of progress that is not complete until we are reunited with Christ. This is called "progressive sanctification." Progressive sanctification is a process by which the Holy Spirit produces in believers a gradually increased likeness to Christ. It begins at the time we are cleansed of our sins and saved by faith and continues throughout our lives on earth. You must train your faith and your spirit to endure the marathon to come. Athletes train to run marathons; they don't just wake up on the day of the event and decide to run a marathon. Nor do they train for a week and are suddenly ready to compete. Training takes time, and in time you will receive the breakthrough you have been praying so earnestly for. Remember, God is always on time, and His timing is perfect, so trust in His timing. Train yourself daily to prepare for the race of faith so you will have the endurance to finish the marathon that will lead to eternity in Heaven. The goal is to win the race of faith and be with our Father in Heaven for all eternity. So, tell me, are you ready to run your race? Father in Heaven, I pray that You will equip every believer with the endurance to run the marathon in pursuit of righteousness. That You will cover them with grace and empower them to continue this journey You have created them to travel. It is in the name of my Lord and Savior Jesus Christ I pray, Amen.

Do not be conformed to this world, but be transformed by the renewal of your mind, that by testing you may discern what is the will of God, what is good and acceptable and perfect.

—Romans 12:2 (NLT)

CHAPTER 5

Conform or Transform?

We live in a world where people have become prisoners of what I like to call "horizontal validation," meaning that we have become prisoners to the opinions and approval of others. This is a weakness for a vast number of people because we find ourselves in alignment with the customs and practices of a life we were not created to live. We are not meant to become the likeness of the world, but instead, we are meant to become more like Christ. The apostle Paul said in the book of Romans 12:2 (NLT), "Do not be conformed to this world, but be transformed by the renewal of your mind, that by testing you may discern what is the will of God, what is good and acceptable and perfect." I want to expound on "vertical alignment" and "horizontal alignment."

Vertical alignment is when you are focused on God. When the Holy Spirit is leading you, it is your internal, spiritual desire to be filled with the presence of God and follow His commandments, to submit and surrender to His will, His control, and His direction. This is allowing the Holy Spirit absolute control over your life. When you are vertically aligned you only seek validation from the One you serve. I remember immediately after I delivered my first sermon, I began to pursue God's approval. I started speaking to God and asking Him if I had said all that He wanted me to say and if my words brought Him glory. I had not yet left the podium and I was already seeking God's approval. Here is the beautiful thing: when you are serving to what He has called you to do, you already have His approval. In my case, it was my humility that was seeking His approval because I wanted to be a good steward of what He called me to do. When you are vertically aligned you are aware of His presence, you can hear His words when He speaks to you. When you are not in alignment with God, your ears will become deaf to His words. The sounds of society will become amplified and will be the only sounds you are able to hear, therefore drowning out the prompts and directions of God.

What you are aligned to determines the trajectory of your life. When you are vertically aligned, you will continue to move forward in the purpose God has for you. When you are horizontally aligned, you will become stagnant by trying to keep up with society. Horizontal alignment is when you are focused on the sins of the world. Following sinful nature is allowing our internal desires to conform and come into alignment with external temptations. This then leads us to be consumed by the temptations of this world. The pictures you project in public are what people see. The pictures you project in private are what God sees. Who are you really? The person you present in private or the person you present in public? Are you someone who projects on social media that you have the perfect marriage but once you return home you and your spouse sleep in separate bedrooms? Are you someone who projects an expensive lifestyle but in secret you are drowning in debt? Or are you someone who publicly appears to have it all together but in private you are falling apart in isolation? What you align to determines if it will be a strength or a weakness.

> **We were created to be original, a pure source, not a copy or a counterfeit version of ourselves.**

When you conform to something you behave according to the conventions or socially acceptable standards. We were created to be original, a pure source, not a copy or a counterfeit version of ourselves. Something that is counterfeit is a fraudulent imitation of the original version. An imitation of something will never have an equal value to the original. If I were to imitate every pastor I have watched online who had a large following, I would be speaking their words and not the words of the Holy Spirit. I would be speaking from sinful nature and selfish ambition, and I would not be led by the source of He who works in me so that His children will receive what He desires for them to receive. I would not be speaking from a place of truth but from a place of lies, imitation, and deceit. We live in a society where people will not wear clothes or shoes that are a counterfeit of the originals. However, we will live a counterfeit life in public just so we can receive the approval of others who are only around us because we make them feel more valued because in their eyes we are less than.

I remember there were times when I would post on social media and I would check the post every ten to twenty minutes like clockwork to see the number of likes the post had received. I was looking for validation in places that would not sustain me, and it only temporarily satisfied me. I speak from a place of truth because I have lived this life as well. This was also a weakness of mine. I was seeking validation in places that could not fulfill my desire to be seen and wanted. I should have abstained from falling deep into the realm of what I like to call "cyber self-worth." Instead, I walked deeper and deeper down the side roads of sin in the opposite direction of where God was trying to take me. God sustains where He remains, so be careful what you abstain from. When you refrain from something you abstain from it. Ensure you abstain from the things that pollute your purity and not from what protects it. It only takes a small dose to pollute what is pure. Only Jesus can cleanse what has been contaminated from sin.

We were created to be a pure source. When you are pure, you are free of any contamination and are not a diluted source of who you were created to be. There is freedom in authenticity. When you are your authentic self, you can speak from a place of truth because you are speaking from authentic experiences that you have encountered throughout your life. Be a pure source and not a diluted source. When something is diluted, it is made weaker in force, content, or value by modification. I was speaking to my coworkers one day when they asked me my opinion on a certain subject. I tried to respond with the most politically correct answer, but the Holy Spirit spoke to me and said, "Opinions are empty without the weight of truth." That was a "drop the mic" moment for the Holy Spirit.

When you begin to form an opinion of the truth, you will take your opinion to your friends, and they will also form their own opinions. This process will continue until the opinions will become the new truth, therefore creating acceptance of the counterfeit and not the source in which the truth comes from.

Will you accept the opinions of who others say you are? Or will you receive the truth of who you are from the source who created you? Will you be a diluted version of yourself? Or will you follow the example of Christ and be led by the Holy Spirit? Conform to the word of God and do not be diluted by the customs and behaviors of the world. You have been transformed by grace through salvation in Jesus Christ. You were transformed into a new creation, not a duplicate of someone else. To be transformed means to make a marked change in one's form, nature, or appearance. A marked change is the difference in behavior or in a situation that shows an obvious or noticeable shift. May I inform you that you will get noticed more by being the new creation that you are if you have accepted Jesus Christ as your Lord and Savior than you would by trying to be a copy of someone else. There is not only freedom in authenticity, but there is strength as well. You will find strength by confidently going forward and being a beacon of light by allowing others to see God's presence through you. It is important to take God with you everywhere you go. The enemy will place obstacles in your way to not make you act out of character but out of calling. Your character is what people deem you to be by the opinions they have developed based on the qualities they have seen you display. In this way, they place you in a box that you were never meant to be held in. Your calling is what God ordained and created you to be, living an authentic life swimming against the ocean currents of the world in a pursuit of righteousness.

You were uniquely created for a specific purpose, calling, and anointing. You cannot fulfill what you were uniquely created to do by being a copy of the world. Do not allow yourself to become a watered-down version of yourself. God cannot work in who you are trying to be; He only can work in who you were created to be. When you are trying to be something else you are combating the work He is trying to do in and through you. Renew your mind and redirect your alignment. When something is renewed it is replaced or repaired. Repair your mind and replace the internal desires to seek horizontal validation with the desire to be aligned vertically with God. Invite God into those places and ask Him to redirect your pattern of thinking. Receive peace in knowing that God has already validated you. Your self-worth, or the way others perceive your worth, will never compare or reach to the heights of your worth with God.

We live in a society where we conform for confirmation. We seek confirmation on how we should live and whether we are valued above what we perceive as our self-worth. Our self-esteem can be a self-inflicted prison. It is one of the driving factors for wanting to adopt the lifestyles that others are projecting. The movie-like life they are projecting to the world seems better than the short story we deem our lives to be. We allow our self-esteem to be the director of our story even though it did not create the story. There is no collaborative effort between the creator and the director in this sense. They present two different creative visions of our stories. Our self-esteem causes us to chase a dream-like life so that we may have glimpses of feeling appreciated and seen. The key word here is "glimpses." A glimpse is a momentary or partial view that can only be perceived briefly or partially. What our internal desires seek can only be given partially before those desires need to be refilled again, which places you in another cycle that binds you in the prison of your emotions. Do not allow your self-esteem to direct the position of your alignment. Shift it to the One who created you and the story you were meant to live out. God knows your story because He created you and had plans for you before you were in your mother's womb (Psalms 123:13–18 [NLT]).

Once your alignment shifts and you are no longer swimming with the current but are now swimming against the current, you begin to lose people you thought would never leave your side. This part of your transition is what I refer to as the "circle cleansing phase." People will begin to slowly fade away because now you are living on a different frequency than they are. You have now figured out your worth in the eyes of God, and now they cannot use you to make themselves feel more valued because you are no longer broken. Not everyone is meant to endure this journey with you. There are people who will encourage your walk of faith and there are people who will try to pull you away from it. God will clear the path and remove any obstacles that will take you away from Him. Stay on the path He has laid down before you and you will be sheltered in His presence. Consider yourself in good company. All the apostles and every other person you read about throughout biblical history swam against the current. They did not conform to the ways of the world but went against it. They were persecuted for living lives of faith and for not following political doctrines that were used to advance the selfish beliefs of others. If the apostle Paul (formerly known as Saul) would have continued to live this way of life we would have missed about 28 percent of the New Testament. It is good to be an original. I encourage you to live a life of authenticity. Allow the world to see the beautiful creation that you are.

Yet in all these things we are more than conquerors through Him who loved us. For I am persuaded that neither death nor life, nor angels nor principalities nor powers, nor things present nor things to come, nor height nor depth, nor any other created thing, shall be able to separate us from the love of God which is in Christ Jesus our Lord.

—Romans 8:37–39 (NLT)

CHAPTER 6

Just Keep Going

When I think about the title of this chapter, I think of one of the most challenging seasons that you may be experiencing. I think of how the difficulties of this season have hit you from every angle. It may seem as if no matter what direction you turn to, there is an immovable object which you cannot move on your own power. There may seem to be an unbearable weight that you can no longer carry. It may seem like you are trapped in a never-ending pattern of being brought to your knees. What if I were to tell you that this is the best position to be in? This position can replenish your strength and refuel your faith. It is amazing how such a submissive posture can bring you power. In this instance there is power in the paradoxes of life. So, when life brings you to your knees, it's OK. Stay in that position and pray. In that submissive posture, submit to God the unbearable weight you are carrying. To submit is to yield to the authority or will of a superior force. Yield to God's authority and allow Him to release you from the weight you have been struggling to carry. We must get out of the pattern of trying to do God's job for Him. We cannot carry what God can carry.

There have been numerous instances in my life when I have tried to carry unbearable weights that I was not designed to carry, such unforgiveness, shame, anxiety, and addiction. The weight I most recent struggled with was unforgiveness. Have you ever found yourself in a situation where you felt betrayed? This betrayal came from a person I did not expect to betray me, and the act of betrayal was something so unimaginable that I felt shocked before anger consumed me. Betrayal became the driver of my emotions, and I was along for the ride. It was exceedingly difficult for me to speak the words "I forgive you." I was trapped in a void of unforgiveness. I had never found myself unable to forgive someone. If I could not speak it from my mouth, I knew that I could not release it from my heart. I knew prayer would be the only way I would be able to release this unbearable weight I was carrying. I prayed and asked God to give me the grace to forgive and to release the weight that was wearing me down.

One day, as I was doing a devotional with a friend, we began to speak about betrayal and unforgiveness. We spoke about the Last Supper, and how the disciples betrayed Jesus Christ before the crucifixion. During this devotional, the Holy Spirit begin to reveal things to me. According to Luke 23:34, while Jesus was on the cross, He cried out to God, "Father, forgive them for they don't know what they are doing." He spoke forgiveness after He was ridiculed. He spoke forgiveness after He was tortured. He spoke forgiveness while He was dying. He forgave with His heart and His mouth in impossible situations. This is the example that we are to follow. Now, I want to point out what the Holy Spirit spoke to me. Not only did Jesus speak forgiveness, but He walked and displayed forgiveness before He spoke it on the cross. During the Last Supper, Jesus spoke to the disciples about betrayal and denial. He told Judas that he would betray Him. He told Peter that He would deny Him, and He said that the disciples would all fall away (Luke 22:7–38 [NLT]). Throughout my life I have heard sermons on this subject, but this part was always overlooked. After He predicted the betrayal and denial, He continued to remain with the disciples. He spent His last moments free in human form with the very disciples who would deny Him and fall away.

Jesus predicted Peter would deny Him, and even with the revelation of betrayal He remained with the disciples. Peter and the other disciples accompanied Jesus to the garden and remained in His presence. Jesus could have easily rebuked the disciples, but He forgave them without even saying it. His actions spoke forgiveness, He walked in forgiveness. When I received this revelation, I received the grace I was seeking. The weight of unforgiveness was lifted. Not only should our words speak forgiveness but our actions should speak forgiveness as well. So, when you tell someone that you love and forgive them, let your actions speak that as well. The enemy wants to derail us from our path. Do not help him knock you off track. Receive the grace and peace of Jesus, pick yourself up, and keep going. Do not dwell in unforgiveness and unfaithfulness, just keep going.

One thing I am certain of is that we all have battles that come in different forms. Your battle may not be unforgiveness. Will you face your battle head-on? Will you press forward fearlessly and full of faith? We are more than conquerors through Christ who loved us (Romans 8:37 [NLT]). When you conquer something, it means that you overcome it. If Christ be for you, it does not matter who or what is against you. You have the power through the Holy Spirit to overcome the hurt and pain; it will not overtake you. Life may cause you to stumble but it will not overcome you. It has already been conquered. Jesus Christ said in the book of John 16:33 (NLT), "I have told you all this so that you may have peace in me. Here on earth, you will have many trials and sorrows. But take heart because I have overcome the world." This means that victory is yours. Claim your victory and break the chains of defeat. No longer will you fall deeper and deeper into the abyss of defeat. Pick yourself up and just keep going. The breakthrough is closer than you think. If you quit now you will miss all the things God wants to do in your life.

I know that life can be difficult sometimes. I know there are times when you are ready to wave the white flag and surrender. Imagine yourself as a prizefighter in a championship match. It seems every plan you came into this fight with is not working. Your opponent knows every move you are attempting to attack with. He counters every punch to perfection, and now you find yourself on the mat and the referee is starting to count. At this moment, you can do one of two things. You can either stay down or get up and keep fighting. When an unexpected hit connects with precision and knocks you down, what will you do? Will you stay down, or will you get up and keep fighting? When a seemingly inescapable sin brings you to your knees and all you can do is dwell in defeat, what will you do? For the Bible says in Proverbs 24:16 (NLT), "The godly may trip seven times, but they will get up again. But one disaster is enough to overthrow the wicked." No matter how many times you get knocked down, pick yourself up and just keep going.

You may have thought the adversary you were facing was too great for you to conquer. The giant before you may have seemed like an immovable force, and you did not feel equipped with the right armaments to battle this giant. If you give the battle to God, He will give you victory over this giant with the armaments you thought were inadequate. I want to remind you of the fight between David and Goliath. Goliath brought fear into the Israelites. His mere presence projected dominance. So dominant was he that he taunted the army day after day, and no one would face him. That is, until David arrived at the camp. With God on his side, David entered battle against Goliath with a sling and a rock (1 Samuel 17:45–51 [NLT]). He did not need a sword or any other weapon to conquer his giant. God gave him victory with the armaments he already had. He walked into battle being who he was created to be, and not a version of something he was trying to be. Therefore, God was able to use him and what he was equipped with to accomplish what others saw as impossible. So throw your rock and take down your giant.

Victory is absolute, but you must claim it with faith. David walked into battle with absolute faith. His faith gave him victory before he threw the rock. When God fights the battle for you, the outcome is already determined. According to 1 Samuel 17:46–47 (NLT), "Today the Lord will conquer you, and I will kill you and cut off your head. And then I will give the dead bodies of your men to the birds and wild animals, and the entire world will know that there is a God in Israel! And everyone assembled here will know that the Lord rescues his people, but not with sword and spear. This is the Lord's battle, and he will give you to us!" The weapon may be formed but it will not prosper, for the giant before you will not overtake you. David and Goliath were in a battle because they were enemies and not allies. When you are engaged in spiritual warfare, it is because the enemy sees you as an opponent and not an ally. This is because you are not in alignment with the enemy. If you were an ally, you would not be in a battle because you would follow the enemy's way of life. Since you are of Christ, you are in opposition. Find joy in your battle. The fact that you are in a battle shows that you are on the right side. Battles only come to adversaries, so continue to fight your battle. The Holy Spirit fights on your behalf and wages war against the flesh daily. Side with the Holy Spirit so that sin will not conquer you.

If you allow God to lead you and go into battle for you, there is nothing that can overtake you. The anxiety, depression, and addiction will be defeated. You can win this fight. This season that you are in will not defeat you. You have come too far to allow yourself to fall back into the temptations that taunt you day after day. The Holy Spirit dwells within you and gives you the power to keep going. No matter what barren lands or deserted places you may find yourself in spiritually or emotionally, He will bring you through them. You can walk through the valleys of the shadows of death and fear no evil because He is with you. There is no longer a need to fear the night that never seems to end. There is no longer a need to retreat from the storm that seems imminent. You do not have to run away and seek shelter back into the very places that had bound you in defeat. God is your refuge; He will shelter you within His presence. He is all you need to overcome any difficult season in your life. Live a victorious life, for you were not created to live anything less.

> **You can walk through the valleys of the shadows of death and fear no evil because He is with you.**

I believe in you, and most importantly, I believe and have faith in the God we serve. He will never abandon you. We are not orphans; we are His children. A father will fight for and protect his children against any danger that arises. There is no enemy that can defeat you if you lean in and trust God. You have already given Him your heart. Allow Him to have the things that mean you harm as well. He does not wish to be separated from His children, He wishes to be in constant relationship with us. I pray that you will be filled with the courage you need to face your giants. That you will be able to approach any battle you may be facing with absolute confidence. That you will find joy in the battles you face because the victory is already yours. I also pray that you will have trust where there was once doubt. Find peace in the chaos that life creates against you. It is in the mighty name of my Lord and Savior Jesus Christ I pray, Amen.

The Lord is my light and my salvation; Whom shall I fear? The Lord is the strength of my life; Of whom shall I be afraid?

—Psalms 27:1 (New King James Version)

CHAPTER 7

Faith in the Valley

Have you ever found yourself in a negative situation, and you couldn't figure out how you got there? Your life seemed to be going in an upward trajectory and you were beginning to find your stride. You started to find success in the areas of your life where there was once failure. You started to see a harvest in places of your life where there was once a famine. Then, without warning, your life slipped into the depths of a place that seemed dark and impossible to escape from. The fact is, at some point in our lives, we have all been in the valley. A valley is a *depressed area* of land between mountains. It is created by erosion or the waste between two mountains by water or ice. Erosion is a *gradual destruction* of something. The valley is the *lowest point* between two high points. Notice the italicized words: "depressed area," "gradual destruction," and "lowest point." Therefore, the valley is dark, and it seems impossible to escape. The valley brings depression from the gradual destruction of the life in which you thought you were headed in an upward direction. It is because of this drastic redirection that you find yourself at your lowest point.

There were times in my life when I've found myself in the valley, and I saw the steep mountain before me, a massive mountain that I did not know how I would have the strength to climb. This mountain was the only way to escape this valley that I had found myself in. So I began to climb out of the valley in pursuit of freedom. During my climb, I would choose the wrong route and fall back into the valley, leaving myself worse off than I was before. No matter how many times I would try to climb to freedom and escape the depths, I would fall back into the valley. My attempts to gain vision in the darkness that would produce fruitful results would be unfruitful. We have a habit of wanting to do things on our own instead of seeking help or guidance. I came to the realization that I was approaching this impossible task without seeking help from the God who makes all things possible. When you are in the valley you have a choice to make. Will you stay in the valley? Or will you have faith and wait on God to move you to the next highest point? I'm not asking you to question whether you desire to remain in the valley. Believe me, I know the valley is not where you want to be. However, if all your attempts to escape are centered around your own strength and understanding, you will remain in the place you are trying to escape from. It is only by faith in God and the

> **When you are in the valley you have a choice to make. Will you stay in the valley? Or will you have faith and wait on God to move you to the next highest point?**

strength that He will give us that we begin to climb out of the valley.

We cannot escape inescapable situations without the God who makes all things possible. It is by the strength that He gives us that we can see past our limitations because He is limitless. We must rely on the guidance and direction of the Holy Spirit. He will guide us on our journey out by showing us the right direction. He will illuminate the path before us that will lead to freedom. In the book of Psalms 119:105 (NLT) it says, "Your word is a lamp to guide my feet and a light for my path." This is what I love about God's word, specifically in the book of Psalms. In this book you will see numerous chapters in which David found himself in circumstances that could be identified as his "valley." Psalms 27 is a chapter that I find to be immensely powerful. When David wrote this chapter he was believed to have been in exile. Biblical scholars are split on whether he was in exile hiding from Saul or if he was about to go into battle with his son Absalom. Whichever side of the spectrum you fall on, one thing we can all agree on is that he would have been deeply troubled. Psalms 27 is broken down in two parts. Verses on through six are his confession, and verses seven through fourteen are his prayer to God. This chapter concludes with a statement that a lot of us have trouble obeying: "Wait patiently for the Lord." David did not allow his present circumstance to change or hinder his faith in God. He did quite the opposite by expressing his confidence in God and seeking refuge in Him. He knew that only God could sustain him in what he was going through. David understood the revelation that we all need to receive: if I wait on the Lord, He will make a way. He will give me strength when I am weak, and peace when I am troubled.

There is a verse in the book of Isaiah 40:31 (NLT) that should be a declaration over our lives: "But those who trust in the Lord will find new strength. They will soar high on wings like eagles. They will run and not grow weary. They will walk and not faint." Trust gives birth to faith. They are not mutually exclusive, and they need one another to exist. So, when you place your trust in the Lord, it will add fire to your faith. It is in that moment when your perspective of the mountain that is before you will begin to change. I would like to give you some key points that I have begun to use, which I am sure will provide results in your journey. When we find ourselves in the pits of our valleys, the first thing we often do is ask why. Why am I going through this? Why is this happening to me? In my career field, when we are tasked to give a brief or receive a brief, the foundation of the brief will be the five W's:

- Who?
- What?
- When?
- Where?
- Why?

It is in those difficult moments that we need to utilize the five W's. Let's unpack this in a very practical way:

- **Who:** Who can I serve or sow a seed in today for you, Lord? Who is it that You will place in my path who needs to hear about you, Jesus? Who needs a word of encouragement?

- **What:** What are You trying to show me during this situation or circumstance? What is the revelation? What are You preparing me for?
- **When:** Lord, I do not know when this will be over, but I trust in You. I know You use everything for good and everything has a purpose. Adversity births purpose, and I submitted to Your process, not mine.
- **Where:** Where is it that You want me to serve today? Lord, I am Your instrument of service and worship. I live to serve Your will and purpose for my life. For You order the steps of the righteous. Send me, Lord, and I will go.
- **Why:** How can I change and recalibrate my "why?" Instead of asking "Why am I going through this?" as a question to God, I will use it as a declaration. Lord, I don't know why I am going through this, but I trust You and I know You will never leave or forsake me. What you bring me to You will see me through. This redirects my faithless "why" into a faithful declaration to God.

I love the opening of Psalms 27. This verse gives me strength and perspective. It is amazing how the word of God can correct our vision. Psalms 27:1 (NKJV) says, "The Lord is my light and my salvation; Whom shall I fear? The Lord is the strength of my life; Of whom shall I be afraid?" Jesus Christ has been the light since light was spoken into the world. He was the light in creation, the light of creation, a light that can never be extinguished. So why should we fear the valley that we are in? For when our Savior shines His light upon us, there is no darkness that can consume us. Our confidence resides in the light while fear hides in the darkness. When we put our faith in God and are led by the Holy Spirit, we are bold and courageous to face the mountains before us. For if Jesus Christ resides in your heart, there is no room for fear. For God did not give His children a spirit of fear. He gave us a spirit of power, love, and sound mind (2 Timothy 1:7 [NLT]).

> **The ascension out of the valley begins with the revelation that you are a new creation.**

The ascension out of the valley begins with the revelation that you are a new creation. You are no longer the person who found comfort in the valley. The old you has passed away, and nothing old can reside in something that is new. You will also need to conduct an inventory of who you allow access to your journey. There will be people who will only see you as the old you and will not accept the rebirth of the new you.

Here is the thing: people who are in the valley see true freedom as a prison. They will attempt to deter you from your ascent by trying to cloud your vision with their perceptions of the direction your life is going. In this season of your life, you must protect your focus. Your focus will determine if you will be led to green pastures or will dwell in dark valleys. If you place your focus on God, there is no circumstance that will overcome you. There is no obstacle or adversary that will cause you to drift from the path that God has placed before you. However, if you find yourself to have drifted away or gone astray, He will find you. You may stray away, but our Lord and Savior will leave the ninety-nine to find the one who went astray (Matthew 18:13 [NLT]). He will come to the valley, take hold of your hand, and lead you out. All you must do is place your faith and your trust in Him. There was a specific verse in Psalms 27:9 (NLT) that caught my attention: "Do not turn your back on me. Do not reject your servant in anger. You have always been my helper. Don't leave me now; don't abandon me, O God of my salvation!" At some point in our lives, we have all been in a place where this verse was our reality. This verse is especially important and provides a doorway for perspective because when we are in the valley and cannot fathom why, the first thought that creeps into our minds is, "Has God left me?" It is one phrase that brought life to this verse for me. In this verse David wrote, "You have *always* been my helper." The word "always" means at all times and on all occasions. God is always with you! He is "who was, who is, and who is to come!" There is no part of your life where He is not with you. We were created to be in fellowship with God, not sin or fear. Being in fellowship with sin and fear is a choice, but being in fellowship with God is our purpose.

As I previously mentioned, we must trust the Lord to show us the right path to ascend the rugged terrain of the mountain before us. In Psalms 27:11 (NLT), we receive this very direction from God: "Teach me how to live, O Lord. Lead me along the right path, for my enemies are waiting for me." When you follow the path the Lord has made for you, He will lead you on a path of righteousness. This path will lead you to less troubled paths and will offer you freedom over your circumstances. Reside in the presence of the Lord and you will continue to ascend without grabbing hold of a loose rock that will result in your downfall back to the valley. I cannot think of a better verse that declares this than Psalms 23:1–4 (NLT): "The Lord is my shepherd; I have all that I need. He lets me rest in green meadows; he leads me beside peaceful streams. He renews my strength. He guides me along right paths, bringing honor to his name. Even when I walk through the darkest valley, I will not be afraid, for you are close beside me. Your rod and your staff protect and comfort me." In the Lord's presence you have provisions, for He is *Jehovah Jireh*. In the Lord's presence there is rest and peace, for He is *Jehovah Shalom*. The Lord sees you and is close beside you, for He is *Adonai El Roi*, "the God who sees me."

For when you go through the valley of the shadow of death, you can go in all power for He who has all power is with you! The same Spirit that raised Jesus Christ from the dead, the same Spirit throughout history that empowered the prophets and apostles of God, is in you! You have power in you! The valley can bring fear if you are not anchored in faith. For if you do not have faith that God is with you, the valley will consume you. Darkness will cover you and the light will be absent, blotted out by despair and discouragement. I have good news for you. Whether or not you see Him and feel Him, He is still there. During those silent moments, that is when He does His greatest work. During those silent moments, He who is the master craftsman is crafting your breakthrough. Therefore, approach every circumstance, storm, or dark valley with faith and confidence. Because the God who sees you is with you and will never leave you. Declare these Scriptures over your life and you will see that light overcomes the darkness. Seek God and He will give you all that you need to ascend to your breakthrough. The valley can no longer hold you if it's time to walk in the freedom that Christ has already given you.

So, Jesus told them this story: "If a man has a hundred sheep and one of them gets lost, what will he do? Won't he leave the ninety-nine others in the wilderness and go to search for the one that is lost until he finds it? And when he has found it, he will joyfully carry it home on his shoulders. When he arrives, he will call together his friends and neighbors, saying, 'Rejoice with me because I have found my lost sheep.' In the same way, there is more joy in heaven over one lost sinner who repents and returns to God than over ninety-nine others who are righteous and haven't strayed away!"

—Luke 15:3–7 (NLT)

CHAPTER 8

Commit to the Climb

In the previous chapter I talked about having faith in the valley, which is also about making the daily commitment to climb out of the valley. Committing to the climb is the next step. The valley is a place of destruction and darkness. It is also the place where God will meet you and strengthen you to condition you for the climb. I once preached a sermon that resonated with me so deeply. It was the story of the Samaritan woman at the well. This is a familiar story in the Bible that shows that Jesus will leave the ninety-nine to find the one who went astray. It shows that you are never too far to be found and redeemed by the grace and love of Jesus Christ. It also shows how the daily climbs we commit to can change our lives. This story takes place on the top of Mount Gerizim, which is about 250 feet in elevation. Therefore, Photini had to physically climb uphill to visit the well to replenish her water. She had to take a journey from the village of Sychar to seek physical nourishment. Little did she know that she would have an encounter that would provide her spiritual nourishment to change the trajectory of her life.

What resonated with me so deeply about this story was that her daily climb was probably the only peace she experienced throughout her day. It was an escape from the constant ridicule and rejection she faced because of her sins. It was also filled with pain, as this midday journey was a constant reminder of the life she had chosen to live. Due to these facts, she chose not to venture on this journey with the rest of the women from her village. You can see that peace and pain resided in the same space. In the midst of her peace was a constant feeling of pain. Every deep breath she took as a result of the heat, and every drop of sweat that streamed down her face, was a reminder of the life she was leading. Every step she took up the mountain to replenish her source of external nourishment depleted her internally. In her daily journey to be refilled, she would lose more than she would gain.

Sychar was the valley she had to ascend out of every single day. This was the place where her identity was determined based on what others declared her to be. Let me pause right here and explain that in this life if we often do not believe we are who God says we are. Instead, we believe we are who others say we are. If we lose sight of our identity in Christ, we will agree with the false identifications of what people have labeled us as. Looking back to the story, Photini's valley was familiar to me. It brought to mind how dangerous sins can become too familiar. In one of its basic definitions, "familiar" can be used to describe a close or intimate relationship. Sin becomes comfortable when it becomes familiar. Similarly, Photini's valley was a familiar place. It was her home, the place she was from and had so intimately known. It was also the place where her sin imprisoned her. It was a familiar walk, a walk that was a reminder of who she was and what she had done, that would lead to her meeting the Messiah who would pardon her sins. She arrived at the mountain a sinner, an adulterous woman, but after her encounter with Jesus she went back as an evangelist, a missionary with a seed to sow that would free her entire region. This is why we cannot escape the valley on our own strength. When we have become comfortable in our valley, the comfort of sin entraps us by showing us the heights of the climb we must ascend to escape from the depths of our valley. It seems like an impossible task that paralyzes our hope and faith of ever being free from the depths we have made our home.

How do we begin to ascend out of the depths of the valley? We have to commit to the climb. We have to make the daily decision to submit to the guidance of the Holy Spirit to lead us on the path out of the valley. If you embark on this journey on your own strength, you will not be able to find firm footing and will soon find yourself back in the valley. For the word of God is the lamp that will light our path. It is the Spirit who leads in all truth that will keep us on the path of righteousness. The Holy

Spirit is our compass that recalibrates our steps when we drift away from the path we are called to walk. The next step is to condition yourself for the climb. We condition ourselves by filling our days with the presence of God in a very practical way by starting each day with prayer and reading God's word. You do not have to do something profound. Just start in a very practical way and commit to it. No one wakes up one day to run a marathon without prior training and conditioning. You have to prepare and condition yourself. You may be able to run only one mile without stopping, but if you keep practicing you will begin to go farther and farther, as long as you do not give up. In the same way, you will not wake up one day without prior training and successfully climb a mountain without feeling the effects of the climb.

Do not be discouraged if you stumble or fall. Do not retreat in shame if you fall back into the valley. If you keep going, you will build endurance for the climb and you will go farther and farther. I have fallen back into the valley more times than I can count. I have stumbled on my climb, and I have fallen flat on my face, but I never gave up. I refuse to allow myself to dwell in the depths of a place that only brings me shame and inflicts pain upon those I love. I refuse to cower in fear of the climb that is before me. God has equipped you with everything you need to make the climb if you will only walk with Him. You are not meant to climb alone, so take the hand of God and He will give you the strength you need to keep going. Find peace in knowing that your climb is a daily decision that God gives you the grace to endure. He will guide your feet to solid ground and your hands to steady rocks. Faith is the strength in your legs that will keep you going. Hope is the air in your lungs that will give you endurance. And God is the source of it all. God will sustain you for the climb. The basic definition of "sustainment" refers to maintaining something for an extended period of time. God sustains us for the mountain that is before us, for it is by His grace that we are equipped to climb.

In my humble opinion, one of the most interesting things about the story in chapter 4 of the book of John is when Jesus Christ revealed Himself as the Messiah. During my preparation for this sermon, I asked myself the question, "Why did Jesus choose Photini to reveal His divine identity to?" I pondered this question for a couple of days, and I eventually saw Photini from a different perspective. If you look deeply into the story, she was a singular person who embarked on a daily journey during a specific time. She would leave the masses in her village to take her walk of solitude to Jacob's well. At that moment, the Holy Spirit revealed to me that she was the one who had gone astray. Jesus Christ could have gone into the village and revealed His identity to the masses, but He chose to find the one before revealing Himself to the many. In fact, He used the one to reveal Himself to the many. If you go even deeper into this story, you will see that once Jesus revealed His identity to Photini, He simultaneously changed her identity as well. Look at this from the outside perspective: As we know, Photini was an outcast in society. She would not have been welcomed in the presence of any societal circle. But when you have an encounter with Jesus Christ, everything changes. For the Scriptures say in John 4:28–30 (NLT), "The woman left her water jar beside the well and ran back to the village, telling everyone, 'Come and see a man who told me everything I ever did! Could he possibly be the Messiah?' So, the people came streaming from the village to see him."

The same people who once rejected Photini prior to her daily climb now listened and accepted her. She climbed the mountain as an adulterous and sinful woman, but she left the mountain as an evangelist to spread the message of the arrival of the Messiah. In the same way Jesus Christ changed the trajectory of Photini's life, He will do the same for you. Photini found her identity in Christ that day. It is important that you do the same, and not listen to the horizontal opinions of others who project a false identity onto you. Identity is the one of the most commonly sought-after things in the world today. The question "Who am I?" has been echoed throughout time and will continue to be, if we do not find our identity in Christ. Our identity comes from the God who created us, not from what others say about us. This is a poisonous lie of the enemy to try and label us as something we were not created to be, a false identification of a less-than identity that was never predestined to be ours. The enemy wants to hinder us in our walks in faith by filling our minds with doubt in our vulnerable moments. We know that a lie and a truth cannot reside in the same space. Neither can a false label and your true identity of who God created you to be.

We cannot allow the horizontal opinions and counterfeit identities people attempt to entrap us in change our vertical worship. Walking in the identity and life you were created to live glorifies God. For if you are doing what you were created to do and are being who you were created to be, He will receive glory from it. You have to make a daily commitment to not open yourself to the external opinions of others and allow them to affect your internal posture. Remember, opinions are empty words without the weight of truth. Because if you do not believe you are who God says you are, you will allow others to tell you who you are. One of the most important

> **Commit to the climb, condition yourself for the climb, and follow the lead of the Holy Spirit as you begin your ascent out of the valley.**

steps in walking in the freedom that Christ has given you is to fully accept your identity in Him. I encourage you to commit to the climb, condition yourself for the climb, and follow the lead of the Holy Spirit as you begin your ascent out of the valley. You were uniquely created for such a time as this. There is no one in this entire world like you. You are one of a kind, so see yourself exactly as God created you. Father in Heaven, I pray that You will reveal to my friend just how important they are to You. Give them peace in knowing their identity is in You, for You created them with such grace and love. Remind my friend that they are a beautiful creation of Yours and that You make no mistakes. It is in the name of my Lord and Savior Jesus Christ I pray, Amen.

You should know the Lord. For everyone, from the least to the greatest, will know me already. And I will forgive their wickedness, and I will never again remember their sins.

—Hebrews 8:10–12 (NLT)

CHAPTER 9

Your Past Does Not Define Your Future

I once read a post on social media that really resonated with me. The post read: "Every saint has a past, and every sinner has a future." I remember seeing this and realizing that my past does not define who I am. The pages may already be written, but that does not determine the following chapters that still remain to be written about my life. There was a sense of encouragement within this post. The very people who now seem like they have it all together had at some point in their lives struggled. Who will you allow to be the narrator of your story? The One who created you, and who knows the entirety of it? Or the mistakes in the past that still seem to be rooted deep within you? We cannot allow our past to continuously pull us back to our old ways of living and thinking. It is as if our past life and the sins we committed have a gravitational pull. (I wonder if Sir Isaac Newton would have ever wondered if gravity would be used as a metaphor to relate gravity to the sins of our past?) I often find myself using gravity as a metaphor for how our past can continue to emerge in hopes of pulling us back into sin. Do not allow your past to pull you back into the depths of what God has pulled you out of.

I know it can sometimes be hard to see the shattered pieces of our lives, pieces that were once a beautiful piece of art painted on a canvas of purpose is now seen as a tainted image that is shown on repeat within our minds. It dominates the way we perceive our future will be. Perception can transform into belief, and that belief can become what you perceive as reality. Where is your focus? Is your focus on the reality you have created? Or is your focus on the life God has created you to live? If your focus is on your past, you will continue to live in the past. You will not be able to escape the depths of your past without grabbing hold of the life preserver of salvation. It is not the sinful acts from our past that hold us in contempt. Once you receive forgiveness and accept Jesus Christ as your Lord and Savior, you are free and are no longer attached to your past or the acts within your past. However, when you allow your focus to drift from the peaceful waters of the present back to the troubled waters of the past, it triggers the emotions of shame, regret, and guilt. These emotions subconsciously trap you within your mind, and you find yourself in a self-imposed prison. You cannot begin to focus on your future until your past no longer has dominion over you. How do you focus on your future? By focusing on the process within the present. When you submit to the present, the process will shape you and prepare you for what God has planned for you in the future.

It is amazing how we can hone our focus on the present and still have our eyes on the future. Because it is in the present that we are prepared for the future. This is something I had to learn along my journey. I have come to understand that if I put all my focus on how God wants to use me right now, that is also preparing me for future service while I am presently serving. God knows you from origin to completion. Therefore, He knows what is to come for you, and He is the only one who can prepare you for whatever plans He has for you. If Jesus Christ is your Lord and Savior, your sins have been expunged from your record. You have been pardoned and are no longer a prisoner of sin. Freedom is yours by the grace of God, so use the freedom that has been given to you to help others who may have struggled with a story like yours. We should allow the past chapters of our lives to be testimonies that can help someone surpass the chapters we have already endured. You are a new creation in Christ, and what once was is no more. Imagine you are walking on a beach and you look back to see the footprints you made in the sand. As you are looking back at your footprints, you see that your footprints are being washed away. What was once present no longer exists.

You are cleansed of your sins in the same manner. The

things you did in your previous life no longer exist. They have been washed away by the blood of Jesus. His sacrifice has purified you of all the sins you have committed throughout your life. He no longer sees or remembers the sins you have committed. In the book of Hebrews 8:10–12 (NLT), it says, "But this is the new covenant I will make with the people of Israel on that day, says the Lord: I will put my laws in their minds, and I will write them on their hearts. I will be their God, and they will be my people. And they will not need to teach their neighbors, nor will they need to teach their relatives, saying, 'You should know the Lord.' For everyone, from the least to the greatest, will know me already. And I will forgive their wickedness, and I will never again remember their sins." Why would you allow your past to dictate your future? God does not remember your past sins, nor does He use them as a prerequisite for the plans He has for you. He does not require a résumé or an application from you to serve in what He has called you to do. You met the qualifications once you surrendered your life to Him through Jesus Christ. For the past has gone by in time and is no longer existing. The thoughts and memories may remain, but that does not mean you have to replay them as daily reminders. Time travel does not exist, and you cannot change what has happened. However, you can determine what happens next. The future represents time or things still to come.

There is more to be written of your life going forward into your future. You may not be able to change the past that has been written, but you can change the future narrative. Let your story be one of victory and deliverance, a story the Holy Spirit can use to free someone who is imprisoned in their past. I am speaking from a place of humility because I was once imprisoned in my past. It was hard for me to believe that God could use someone such as me. I believed that my sins would disqualify me from being able to be used by God. This is what happens when we try to make decisions for God. I was deciding how He would use me without even allowing Him the opportunity to show me Himself. I was building a prison of doubt and disbelief, made from bricks of discouragement. My faith was diluted. I spoke trust, but my actions projected doubt. I knew my walk of faith could not be sustained if I continued down this path. It was time to surrender and ask God to strengthen my faith. I had to relinquish control of my vulnerabilities and weaknesses. I had to release my doubts of what I believed my self-worth to be and accept that I am a child of God.

What are you holding on to? What do you need to relinquish and release to God? Whatever it may be, it will not separate you from the love of God. He has accepted you just as you are, and the Holy Spirit will begin to intercede and will reshape you into a new creation. This book is proof that I believe in what God wants to do in my life. This book was a prophetic message of how I would serve God and help others to not make the same mistakes I have made. I could have allowed my past to deter me and keep me from stepping into His promises. I am no longer bound and anchored to the depths of my past. I have embarked on a journey where the route is not clear but the destination is certain. I want my presence to be proof not only of God's existence but of the fact that He can use anyone, regardless of the past they were released from. My life will be a transparent testimony to those who are struggling to endure. A testimony is evidence or proof of something. It is also a public recounting of a religious conversion or experience. What if your testimony is currently being developed for mass consumption, to be consumed by those who would consider themselves to be your cellmates in the prison of your past, as if they have a firsthand account of the life you've lived because of the similarities between their past and yours? Let your testimony be an aroma of freedom and deliverance that would satisfy the pallet of those who are seeking redemption.

Allow the love of God to be all the justification you need to accept the future that He has in store for you.

Allow the love of God to be all the justification you need to accept the future that He has in store for you. There are no words that can be written that could capture the essence of the love God has for you. His love is deeper than any ocean and vaster than any horizon. Our minds cannot begin to comprehend the love He has for us. It is the most genuine and pure form of love that can be seen and felt throughout all biblical history. He sent His one and only Son to die for a world that did not deserve grace or mercy. You should find freedom in knowing that He sacrificed His Son for the sins of the world. Therefore, if God was willing to make this sacrifice, there is nothing that you can do to separate yourself from Him. God does not walk away from us; we walk away from Him. It is because of this fact that we can repent and receive redemption for our sins. In biblical context, to repent means to turn back to God. Because of this, when you repent, two things happen. First, you have turned back to God and your life has been redirected. Second, your life has shifted and your eternal position has changed. You were once heading in the same direction of the world and had submitted to the position of sin. Now your name is in the Lamb's Book of Life, and you are moving in the direction of the life you were created to live. Repentance is the spark that can change not only your life but your eternity as well. So, turn away from your past, turn away from the things that caused you pain and made you feel unworthy of His love. Jesus Christ displayed compassion and love through the most traumatic event in biblical history. During the crucifixion, He prayed for the very people who mocked and ridiculed Him. This takes a type of love that has no comparison.

We all fall at times, and we all have a past. The fall is temporary unless you decide to remain in your valley. The moments in our lives are temporary unless we decide to remain in them. Each day passes away to give birth to a new day. So allow your past to pass away to give birth to the present. In the book of Matthew 6:34 (NLT), Jesus says, "So don't worry about tomorrow, for tomorrow will bring its own worries. Today's trouble is enough for today." Jesus did not say to worry about yesterday and today. He did not say to worry about yesterday, today, and tomorrow. Jesus said to worry about today—and today only. He was informing us to live in and focus on the present. When a higher percentage of our focus is on the past and the future, it is easy to be overcome by the worries of the present. Release the past, live in the present, and trust God with the future. I highly encourage daily prayer and quiet time with God. It is during this time that you can release all that has plagued you. This is when you can pray and seek the grace that only God can give you to release the things that are impossible to let go of. This is what He wants you to do. He wants to be in communion with you, and He wants you to come to Him for all things. Do not be afraid to go to the Father in the name of the Son to earnestly seek freedom. Then allow the Holy Spirit to empower you to walk in freedom.

The days of being enslaved and bound in the dungeons of your past are over. It is time to shake off the chains that have been broken. I know you may be about to walk in unfamiliar places, but seek refuge in the person who created those places. There should be a fire of excitement beginning to burn inside of you. Walking into something new can be scary, but it also brings excitement of the possibilities to come. There is a new life in front of you and it is filled with the plans you were created to conduct in service to God. Your exodus from the past is the first step after salvation in figuring out who you were created to be. The valleys you were in seemed as if they were endless, but now you are beginning to see the promised land, the place where God wants to meet you and do His greatest work in your life. God, I pray for my friend. I pray You will break the chains that shackled them in the prison of their past. I pray that You will knock down all the walls that surround their spirit. I pray that the doors to their mind, heart, and spirit will open to You. If You are a part of their future, their future will be blessed, for You bless where You are present. I love You, and I thank You, in the name of my Lord and Savior Jesus Christ I pray, Amen.

For the Lord is the Spirit, and wherever the Spirit of the Lord is, there is freedom.

—2 Corinthians 3:17 (NLT)

CHAPTER 10

Freedom

When you hear the word "freedom," what is the first thing that comes to your mind? What is it in your life that you desire freedom from? Freedom is the state of not being imprisoned or enslaved. It is liberation from the power of another. Is there an area in your life where you have experienced liberation? Or does it seem as if freedom is a foreign word that is a world away from the desolate life you cannot escape? I was once in this deserted place where I found myself begging God for freedom. Looking back at that moment, I can see that I was oblivious to the fact that I was already free. I developed every excuse within my mind for how freedom was impossible for someone like me. This is what the enemy does. He attempts to entrap our minds and blind us to the freedom that we already have through Jesus Christ. This reminds me of a passage of Scripture in the Bible. The Scripture I am referring to is about the paralyzed man at the pool of Bethesda. This man had been a resident of this pool for thirty-eight years. This place of hopelessness became his residence. I know this must have seemed like an inescapable eternity for him. Jesus approached the man and asked him if he wanted to be healed. Not realizing that freedom from paralysis was standing right in front of him, all he could do was make excuses for why he could not be healed. As in John 5:7 (NLT), "'I can't, sir,' the sick man said, 'for I have no one to put me into the pool when the water bubbles up. Someone else always gets there ahead of me.'" Jesus went on to heal the man by telling him to get up, pick up his mat, and walk (John 5:8 [NLT]).

Before salvation, we are paralyzed in sin, unable to

move or walk out of it on our own power. It is not until the Holy Spirit convicts us of our sin and leads us to Jesus that we are able to get up and walk in freedom. Jesus told the paralyzed man to pick up his mat because he would not be returning to that place. The man previously could not be liberated from the place where healing was absent because the healer was not present. Once the healer arrived, he was liberated by the liberator. It takes a tremendous amount of patience to wait in one place for thirty-eight years for a miracle. Sometimes it is our patience that prevents us from walking in freedom. This is because we often deem our timeline to be more important than the timeline of God. We desire instant miracles and breakthroughs. If things do not align with our timeline, our immediate response is that God must have abandoned us. Our lack of patience prevents us from allowing ourselves to see the freedom we currently have. Our expectation of freedom is this massive miracle. Do we want freedom? Or do we want a show? You receive freedom in the same way you receive salvation. Faith is the key to the door that unlocks everything that God has in store for you. "Faith is being certain of what you hope for and certain of what you do not see" (Hebrews 11:1 [NLT]).

It is not the lack of patience that is holding you back from experiencing freedom. It is something you have kept hidden deep within the depths of yourself, refusing to release it. There is freedom in confession if you just let go of what you have refused to release. When you keep your struggles private, they begin to become your identity. The longer you keep something within you, the more it becomes a part of you. You will be amazed to find how freeing it will be if you are able to offload the cargo of pain that has been stowed away in your soul. Surround yourself with community and people who can help you with accountability. Even Jesus Christ was surrounded with community. He did not go through His ministry alone. So why should you go through life alone? Private problems cannot be solved with private solutions. Do you desire mercy or secrecy? Sins that

> **Faith is the key to the door that unlocks everything that God has in store for you.**

remain in the dark will keep you in the dark as well. According to Proverbs 28:13 (NLT), "People who conceal their sins will not prosper, but if they confess and turn from them, they will receive mercy." Therefore, repent and redirect away from isolation, and seek God and community. Community can help you begin to release the weight that has been wearing you down.

Coming together in agreement with the body of Christ through prayer will produce results. As in James 5:16 (NLT), "Confess your sins to each other and pray for each other so that you may be healed. The earnest prayer of a righteous person has great power and produces wonderful results." There is healing in revealing the very thing that has crippled your walk in freedom. Have you ever been fishing, and you caught a fish and released it because it wasn't worthy to keep? This is how you should approach the things within you that are hard to release. You should do what I refer to as "confess and

> **Community can help you begin to release the weight that has been wearing you down.**

release." No sin or act from our past is worthy of keeping, nor is it a trophy worthy of being put on display. When we confess our sins to God and receive forgiveness, this is the moment we should release them as well. As found in 1 John 1:9 (NLT), "But if we confess our sins to him, he is faithful and just to forgive us of our sins and to cleanse us from all wickedness." After you receive forgiveness from God, do not forget to forgive yourself. You have received a pardon and have been exonerated from your sins by the sacrifice of Jesus Christ. Exoneration is the act of officially absolving someone from blame and vindication. Jesus lived a perfect life so that He could become sin so that we may be absolved of our sins and transgressions if we repent. It is time to subdue and bring under control the things that have held you captive. Are you ready to walk in freedom and experience the full goodness of God?

What do your actions speak? I know it is easy to speak about freedom, but do your actions display freedom? Do you approach each day that God blesses you to live in creation with a purpose to walk in freedom? I wrote a sermon called "Freedom or Imprisonment." In this sermon, one of my points was that freedom is given by Christ but it is kept by choice. God blessed all of humanity with the freedom of choice. We have the freedom to choose every action and word that leaves our body. We have the freedom to also choose to serve God, as well as the type of life we will live. You may already know this, but we tend to choose things that hold some sort of reverence. We choose to serve God because we have a genuine love and reverence for God. Therefore, when you freely choose to surrender your life to God by accepting Jesus Christ as your Lord and Savior, you also have the choice to freely walk away from the pain that has become your prison. You no longer must blindly wander the wilderness of sin. The endless desert of despair is no longer a cage that can hold you because the key that is freedom can unlock any door. The addiction, childhood trauma, and abuse can no longer hold you. It is time to make a declaration of freedom and independence from the past that was inescapable. You do not need a plethora of signatures to bind this declaration. The sacrifice of Jesus Christ was the final declaration and is the only signature required to receive freedom. For the signature was written in the blood of the Lamb which purifies and cleanses us of all unrighteousness.

Our sins are washed away as the night makes way for the day. We should find joy in the new day and release the sorrows of yesterday. Internalizing the regrets and sorrows of yesterday closes the door to freedom. When you internalize something, it becomes part of your nature by unconscious assimilation. Do not allow these things to remain in your mind and control your thoughts. What you feed your mind matters. Some things are meant to nourish you and will allow your mind to grow and flourish. Thoughts that are negative in nature will repress you and take over every thought that was once pure. When regret and shame become your nature, it also becomes your identity. Be careful what you unconsciously feed your mind because it will become what you consciously seek. Sigmund Freud believed that the conscious mind contains all the thoughts, memories, feelings, and wishes of which we are aware at any given moment. The unconscious mind is a reservoir of feelings, thoughts, urges, and memories that are outside our conscious awareness[1] (McLeod 2015). Consciously fill your mind with God's word so that in times of need your mind will unconsciously seek His word by default. The more you fill your mind with His word, the more your mind will seek it in those silent times when your mind tends to wonder.

I remember when I was dealing with my porn addiction, it seemed as if freedom would never come. I remember asking God, "Why am I this way?" Not only did I feel as if I was imprisoned within the sins of the flesh, but I felt like I was in solitary confinement. Watching porn is something that is done in isolation and in solitude. There is no freedom in anything you choose to do that has to be done in isolation. I isolated myself because I did not want anyone to know the perverse things I was choosing to fill my time with. The reality of porn use is that it gives you a momentary euphoric sense of satisfaction that is immediately followed by shame. How could I feel anything other than shame? I was so deep into this addiction that

---

1 S. A. Mcleod, "Freud and the Unconscious Mind," *Simply Psychology* (blog), 2015, www.simplypsychology.org/unconscious-mind.html.

I began to become numb to the shame. I found myself in the middle of an ocean with waves crashing down until I was forced underwater. This addiction was like a weighted block tied to my body that was causing me to sink into deeper and darker waters. I was in danger of drowning and losing my life to this addiction. It almost cost me everything that God had blessed me with before I even realized He was blessing me. He blessed me with a wife who would support me regardless of the amount of pain I caused her. How could I allow something so impure and distasteful to share a space with a woman who was so beautiful physically and spiritually?

It was in isolation that I had some of the darkest moments of my life. Wouldn't it be like God to use the very thing that you filled with sin to bring you into the light? In the isolation where I would normally fulfill the desires of the flesh, the Holy Spirit found me and carried me to the door of salvation. Jesus was there with open arms to welcome me. On April 4, 2021, my life changed forever. This was a day that I will never forget for the rest of my life. I saw and felt freedom for the first time. I also became instantly and spiritually aware of the type of sinful life I was currently living. The Holy Spirit wasted little time in convicting me of my sins and made it abundantly clear that I was a sinner. I remember saying that prayer of salvation, and I immediately started to delete phone numbers I shouldn't have had and unfollowed women on Instagram whom I shouldn't have been following. I began to develop a pattern of daily prayer and devotion. I wanted to fill myself increasingly with the word of God and His presence. I never wanted to lose that feeling of freedom that was more euphoric than porn ever was in my life. I encourage you to never lose your faith in freedom. Regardless of how deep you think you are sinking and how dark things may seem, God can find you. The Holy Spirit found me in my hotel room, in total isolation. There is nowhere you can go where He can't find you as well. As I said before, there is freedom in submission. When you freely give up and surrender to God, then you will receive the freedom for which you have desperately desired.

When you walk in freedom you walk in favor covered by the grace of forgiveness. You are a child of God, and nothing will separate you from the love He has for you. This is not an excuse to freely commit sin. Sin entraps you from righteousness. We already know that standing in sin is like standing in quicksand. The more you move in it, the faster you will sink. You were created to be a beacon of light in a shadowy world. The light that comes from you will be seen as bright by some and as dim to many others when you straddle the fence between freedom and imprisonment of sin. Go deeper into fellowship with the Holy Spirit and allow Him to ignite the flame in your lamp so that it will burn more brightly. Then your light will be seen by all. Those who hold their lanterns are always on watch and are waiting for the coming of the Lord. Therefore, keep your light burning and do not let sin extinguish it. Just as a lighthouse is a guide for ships traveling in the dark, your light will be a guide for those who are traveling in the darkness of sin. The brighter you burn, the light will begin to overtake the darkness. Jesus Christ is the light of the world. A light that no darkness can consume. Once you have surrendered to Him and have given Him your heart, His light is now in you.

Do not allow the darkness of sin to enter the temple of the Holy Spirit and extinguish the light and flame that is within you. To extinguish means to cause a fire or light to cease to burn or shine; to put an end to or destroy. When we receive salvation, we receive the baptism of the Holy Spirit and of fire. Let your flame burn brightly and let your light be a beacon of peace, faith, and love. Be the example and follow the example of Jesus Christ. When the Holy Spirit consumes you, He removes you. Because we sometimes become the barrier to the work He wants to do in and through us. We rebel against surrendering to what He wants to do in our lives so that we can experience the reality of freedom. True freedom begins when your rebellion ends. Lean in and allow the Holy Spirit to change you and lead you to freedom. For the Holy Spirit is the Spirit of truth who leads in all truth to the one who is the truth, the way, and the life. You have tried so many things in your life. You have tried to fill the emptiness within you with things that have caused the void to grow deeper. Try Jesus instead, and allow Him to fill you with the Holy Spirit. For He will fill you and sustain you. The things of the world will need to be refilled because they will only satisfy you temporarily. Today is the day when your life changes. There is no better time than right now to be free and live a life filled with God's love.

If we are going to take hold of the freedom that has been paid in full, we must walk this life with God. He created us and He knows every part of us. We are a creation of the Most High. Therefore, we must walk this life with the Creator. If we do not, it is the same as trying to build a house without working with an architect. They know how to efficiently strengthen the foundation and every pillar of the house so that, no matter what comes against it, it will stand firm in the face of adversity. We must also walk in the Spirit daily. Going through this life without the Holy Spirit is the same as going to a new destination without having any directions to reach that destination. Relying on our own strength and intellect will cause us to drift into deep waters, offtrack and disconnected from God and where we are supposed to be in life. We can't walk this life without the Creator who has the blueprint of our lives and has the directions of where He wants us to go. In this moment, I want you to think of parallel lines. When you live a life led by the Holy Spirit, your life does not intersect with the secular ways of the world. However, when you are driven by the flesh, the lines intersect. Your life crosses into the thresholds of the world and is at risk of the impurities of sin that pollute what God has made pure. Freedom is yours. I know it seemed that it would never happen. My heart beats in excitement and joy for the freedom that you will receive. I know what it is like to be bound in chains I once saw as unbreakable. We serve the Lord of restoration, and He can make all things whole again. The hidden cracks and broken pieces in our lives are made whole within Him. It is time, my friend, to take your first step in freedom. Lord, I pray for my friend that You will fill them with Your Spirit and empower them to walk in the freedom that we have through Jesus Christ. Shower my friend with Your love and peace, and give them a grace to release the pains of their past. I declare in faith that this will be a season of freedom and deliverance for whomever reads this. It is in the name of my Lord and Savior Jesus Christ I pray, Amen.

If you openly declare that Jesus is Lord and believe in your heart that God raised him from the dead, you will be saved. For it is by believing in your heart that you are made right with God, and it is by openly declaring your faith that you are saved.

—**Romans 10:9–10 (NLT)**

CONCLUSION

My deepest desire is that my story will show you that no matter where you come from, an no matter what you have done in your life, you are reachable and worthy of being saved. God loves you so much, and He has always been with you. I know it is hard to believe when you are in the dark and drowning in your own tears. I know it seems as if He does not hear your voice, even when you scream out in pain until you can no longer produce words. When you are trying to stay above water, and no matter how hard you try, you continue to sink, when you are struggling to live above the surface of your anxiety and despair, all you need to do in those moments is to call out to Him. He sees every tear and knows all the pain that you are holding inside of you. To release it would mean that you would be more vulnerable than you would want to be. You must remember that His power works best in your weaknesses. There is no part of your life that He cannot make strong. There is no part of your life that He cannot restore. Deliverance is available for all who call on His name. Healing is available for all who seek His face. Peace is available for all who seek His presence and remain in His presence. My friend, you are a child of God. You—yes, you. He knows you by name. He desires an intimate relationship with His children. The question is, do you desire this as well? If you do, He will never leave you or forsake you. There is no valley so deep that He cannot find you. No matter how dark your life may seem to be, He will save you from it. There are no words that can capture the true essence of who He is and what He is in our lives. There are no words that can capture the totality of God, but there is one thing we do know: He sent His only Son to die for you and me. This was a sacrifice that can never be repaid by our actions. He only desires our love and faith in Him. He desires to be with us and to have a relationship with us. He who died a criminal's death was not deserving to die in this way, but He did so that we can have freedom!

His sacrifice was an act that can never be repaid, but I will spend my life honoring God and declaring the name Jesus Christ as the Messiah, and my Lord and Savior, everywhere I go. We repay His love by spreading the message of His love. Love begets love, and He is love. My heart longs for the day when I will hear His voice say, "Well done, thy good and faithful servant." My soul anxiously waits in excitement for the day when I will see His face, when I can look and see a love, peace, and grace that words cannot capture. His presence is all these things, and He is proof that it all exists in this time, even when it seems as if it is extinct. His mercy endures forever, and this means there is nothing He won't forgive, if you allow Him to forgive you. There are moments when we refuse to forgive ourselves. If we can't forgive ourselves, then we restrict the forgiveness of those who wish to forgive us because we cannot fully accept it. This prohibits us from fully receiving the forgiveness of God. His grace is sufficient for all our needs, so let go of the weight. Let go of the shame and regret, and receive with open arms and an open heart the forgiveness He has for you. I know the mountain before you seems too high to climb, but the Holy Spirit conditions and strengthens you for the climb to freedom. My friend, you have started your climb. Keep climbing and keep going one step at time. God is with you. Let the Holy Spirit guide you and lead you to the best part of your life. What lies before you is far greater than what is behind you.

One day you will look back at the perilous journey you have endured, and you will realize that God was there with you the entire time. You will be stronger because of it, and you will help others through your story. Your testimony will be a story of perseverance and freedom to those who, like me and you, believed they would never experience it. I am better now because of my journey, and I pray that you are also, and that you will see your journey as a redemptive story to be shared with the hopeless so that they will be filled with hope. As I write this, I write it with a smile on my face and a heart filled with the joy of the Holy Spirit because I know that He can lead you into freedom too. I know what is to come over your life. This book symbolizes freedom and deliverance through Jesus Christ. Every word you have read has brought you a step closer in the direction of freedom. This book has been leading you to this very moment when you will accept Jesus as the Lord and Savior of your life. Open your heart to Him and He will live within you, shining His light upon you. It is time to make a decision that will change the trajectory of your life. You have wanted to be free for so long; now is the moment to take a step in the only direction that will provide you what you so desperately desire.

I can't think of a better way to end this chapter of my life than by allowing you to begin a new chapter of your life. It is time to rewrite your story, and if you are so willing, to begin a new chapter of your life today, in this moment. For if you say this prayer aloud and believe it in your heart you will be saved. For Romans 10:9–10 (NLT) says, "If you openly declare that Jesus is Lord and believe in your heart that God raised him from the dead, you will be saved. For it is by believing in your heart that you are made right with God, and it is by openly declaring your faith that you are saved." Say the following prayer, and your life will forever be changed:

Father in Heaven,

I come to You from a place of humility to confess to You that I am a sinner. I'm sorry for the life that I have lived. I repent my sins and turn back to You. Jesus Christ, I believe You died for my sins and rose again in all power and might. I surrender to You, Lord. Cleanse and purify me of my sins. My life is Yours to change and reshape me into what You created me to be. I accept You as Lord and Savior of my life. Holy Spirit, come live inside me and make me Your dwelling place. Teach me to be more like Jesus Christ every day so that I may follow His example by living a life that glorifies God. I am Yours; my mind, heart, and spirit are Yours. In Jesus's name, Amen.

If you just said this prayer, you are a new creation. Your new life begins now, and freedom is yours. You can now begin to see who you were truly created to be if you surrender all control to God. No matter what has happened in your life or what you have done, it has all passed away. Release the regret and shame that has haunted you and accept the new life you now have in Christ. I hope this book provided you with a renewed sense of faith and hope.

It is my sincerest desire to reach someone in hopes of redirecting them from a life filled with regret and shame. I can now say in all faith that God has delivered me from things I didn't think I would ever be delivered from. He can do this for you as well, if you allow Him to. Your best days are ahead of you if you allow God to take control and go before you. Your sins, transgressions, and iniquities have been nailed to the cross. They are no longer attached to you or reside in God's memory. I want you to see your past as footprints in the sand that are washed away by the living water that Jesus provides to all who believe in Him. The story of my life that I have captured on these pages was a journey of healing. Never in my life would I have guessed that I could be so vulnerable and open to sharing the things in my life that I desperately wanted to forget, the things I wanted to be free of and never look back at. However, I had a burning desire in me to author this book. If I could prevent one person from traveling down the side roads of addiction, shame, and regret, then it would all have been worth it. I love you, and I thank you for spending time with my testimony. God bless you, and may He continue to prosper you for the rest of your life.

ACKNOWLEDGMENTS

I would have never dreamed that I would be an author, that I would be sharing my life story with the world. This can only be God, and I know this is a reality because He opened the door for this to happen. First and foremost, I give all glory and praise to God. For without Him, and His son, Jesus Christ, I would not be here today. I did not write a single word in this book without the guidance and direction of the Holy Spirit. This book is a true testament that if you believe in God, all things are possible in Him. I did not come this far in life without God or the people He placed in my path to help me along the way.

To my wife, Sheryl: Sweet Pea, your constant support and sacrifice has not gone unnoticed. You have given up so much so that I may be in a position to be obedient to wherever God sends me. I thank you from the bottom of my heart. He designed you for me, and me for you. There is no doubt that I am who I am today because of you. I honor you, and I celebrate you for being the best part of me. Being your husband is one of the greatest honors of my life. I love you.

To my grandmother Delores Ramey: Thank you for raising me, and for showing me a true example of what faithfulness to God is. It is because of your constant prayers that I am here today. I honor you, and I love you. I hope I will continue to make you proud.

To my grandfather Robert Ramey: Thank you also for raising me. I wish you could be here with us, but you are in a better place, in Heaven. Save a place for me. I cannot wait until we meet again. I love you.

To my mother, Mattie Ramey: Thank you for giving birth to me. I know it was not easy having a son at the age of twenty while being enrolled in college. You missed out on your college degrees because of me. This is why I chose to not only pursue my undergraduate degree but also my graduate degree. All of my accomplishments thus far have been fueled by your sacrifice. I love you.

To the men who were fathers in my life—Byron and Parnell: Thank you for filling this vacant spot in my life. I appreciate all of the wisdom and guidance you have given me throughout the years. I am the man I am today because you taught me to be so. I love you both, and I cannot thank God enough for all you have done for me.

To my beautiful aunts Priscilla, Rhonda, and Sharon: Thank you for being the best aunties I could possibly ask for. I pray that God will continue to bless you and keep you. I hope that I have—and will continue to—make you proud.

To my brothers Brandon, Darius, and Cyrus, and to my sisters Shankira and Miracle: Being your older brother has been one of the greatest honors of my life. I hope that my life has been a positive example for you all to follow. I look forward to all that the future holds for you.

To my cousins Adrianna, Ari, Quan, Devin, Kentrell, Marlowe, and so many more to name: I pray that God will keep you and bless you. That in His will, you will have a blessed and prosperous life. I am proud of all of you, and I hope that you will love God as much as He loves you.

To my Delmundo family—Rex, Mama Jaquie, Richie, Rhianna, and our adopted Auntie Dhonna: Thank you for welcoming me into your family. Not only did I receive an amazing wife but I also received an amazing family. I am proud to be a part of your family, and I am grateful to have each of you in my life.

To my Covering, Apostle Loutricia Lee: God knew that I needed you on the path that He created me to walk. This book is not only a reflection of my obedience to Him but it reflects your obedience to Him as well. Because you said yes to Him, God led you to me, and I am extremely grateful to have you as a mentor on the path God created for me.

To my sister in Christ, Vallery Traylor: Thank you for listening to my many sermons and notes that I would prepare throughout the weeks. By you giving me some of your time, it allowed for the gifts God put within me to be nourished and grow to where they are now. Thank you for also taking care of my grandmother.

To my brothers in Christ, Drew, Gary, Blayne, and Danny: Thank you for being a constant and consistent presence of encouragement in my life, and for all the opportunities you have given me to do what God created me to do. Also, for your constant fellowship, mentorship, and friendship. I pray that God will continue to bless, protect, and watch over you and your families.

To my sailors, Emily, Jacques, Kokou, Shilong, Tevin, Micco, and Domingo: In the time I have spent with you all, you have taught me the value of leadership and stewardship. I have grown as a leader and have learned the importance of stewardship by watching each of you grow and ascend into your true potential that has no limits. I pray that each of you will serve the purpose God has placed you on this earth to fulfill. You are a unique and special group of people. Remember: with faith, all things are possible.

To Anna Krusinski: Thank you for helping me get my story to the world. I thank you from the bottom of my heart for approaching our partnership with care and complete humility. This process has not felt as a business partnership but that you genuinely care for helping others. There is no way I could leave you off this list. God chose you to help me through this process and to be the bridge for my testimony to reach those who are in need of encouragement. I truly thank you, and God bless you.

ABOUT THE AUTHOR

CHRISTOPHER D. RAMEY was born and raised in Waynesboro, Mississippi. He is a lieutenant in the United States Navy where he has served on active duty for eleven years. Christopher is fully committed to serving his Lord and Savior, Jesus Christ, which has led him to be the pastor of Hallelujah Gospel Church, a nondenominational military-based church service on US Naval Support Activity Naples, Italy, where he currently resides with his wife, Sheryl Sullivan.

www.ingramcontent.com/pod-product-compliance
Lightning Source LLC
Chambersburg PA
CBHW060830050426
42453CB00008B/641